Plant-Based
BUDDHA BOWLS

100 RECIPES FOR NOURISHING
ONE-BOWL VEGAN MEALS

Kelli Foster

HARVARD
COMMON
PRESS

Inspiring | Educating | Creating | Entertaining

Brimming with creative inspiration, how-to projects, and useful information to enrich your everyday life, Quarto Knows is a favorite destination for those pursuing their interests and passions. Visit our site and dig deeper with our books into your area of interest: Quarto Creates, Quarto Cooks, Quarto Homes, Quarto Lives, Quarto Drives, Quarto Explores, Quarto Gifts, or Quarto Kids.

First Published in 2021 by The Harvard Common Press, an imprint of The Quarto Group, 100 Cummings Center, Suite 265-D, Beverly, MA 01915, USA.
T (978) 282-9590 F (978) 283-2742 QuartoKnows.com

The Harvard Common Press titles are also available at discount for retail, wholesale, promotional, and bulk purchase. For details, contact the Special Sales Manager by email at specialsales@quarto.com or by mail at The Quarto Group, Attn: Special Sales Manager, 100 Cummings Center, Suite 265-D, Beverly, MA 01915, USA.

25 24 23 22 21   1 2 3 4 5

ISBN: 978-1-59233-950-1

Digital edition published in 2021
eISBN: 978-1-63159-879-1

Library of Congress Cataloging-in-Publication Data

Foster, Kelli C., author.
Plant-based Buddha bowls : 100 nourishing one-bowl vegan meals / Kelli Foster.

ISBN 9781592339501 (trade paperback) | ISBN 9781631598791 (ebook)
1. Vegan cooking. 2. One-dish meals. 3. Cookbooks.
LCC TX837 .F67 2021 (print) | LCC TX837 (ebook) | DDC 641.5/6362--dc23

LCCN 2020049690 (print) | LCCN 2020049691 (ebook)

Design: Allison Meierding
Photography: Maria Siriano

Printed in China

The information in this book is for educational purposes only. It is not intended to replace the advice of a physician or medical practitioner. Please see your health-care provider before beginning any new health program.

For Owen

Contents

Introduction
VEGAN BUDDHA BOWLS

Why plant-based bowls? For me, the answer is simple: they are the most satisfying and easiest way I know to create a meal that's all about feel-good food. And by that, I mean the foods that make me feel good because they're healthy and nourishing, and also because they're just plain delicious.

I'm a firm believer that food is one of life's greatest joys. I also know that the food we put in our bodies plays an extremely big role in our health and the way we feel. We don't have to choose between one or the other. It is absolutely possible to have both at the same time, and I want to show you how.

My mission with this book is to marry both ideas of feel-good food together with 85 delectable vegetable-forward recipes for plant-based Buddha bowls—plus 15 additional recipes for sauces and extras that you can add to the bowls or use in creating your own bowls. The recipes will take you from breakfast through dinner, and even to dessert, leaving you with wholesome meals to nourish your body and soul.

Whether you're trying to limit meat consumption in favor of more vegetables and whole grains, you're new to adopting a plant-based lifestyle, or you've been following a plant-based diet for years, this book is for you. These bowls are a fun and easy way to eat a little of everything, provide a range of necessary nutrients throughout the day, and are the tastiest approach I know to fuel your body with wholesome and satisfying meat-free meals.

WHAT ARE BUDDHA BOWLS? (AND WHY ARE THEY SO NUTRITIOUS AND DELICIOUS?)

But first, maybe we should recap. Because what exactly are Buddha bowls, anyway? They're often referred to by a variety of names—including power bowls, abundance bowls, and bliss bowls, to name a few—but no matter what you know them as, Buddha bowls are one-bowl meals loaded with a variety of wholesome, real-food ingredients, designed to fuel and nourish your body. They come with the promise of a down-to-earth meal that is good, and good for you—because, like I said, food is meant to be enjoyed.

Each bowl starts with a base, like whole grains, noodles, or vegetables, then gets topped with a whole lot of vegetables, both cooked and raw, followed by a plant-based protein, like beans or lentils, tofu, tempeh, or nuts, before getting finished off with a dressing, sauce, or broth. All of these ingredients are piled into an overflowing bowl for an easy, nourishing meal. To break it down, Buddha bowls are a well-balanced mix of protein, vegetables, and healthful fats that nourish you with a hearty, satisfying meal. In this book, you'll find a versatile mix of stress-free, healthy, plant-based Buddha bowl recipes for breakfast, lunch, dinner, and a little something sweet to finish off the day.

WHAT EXACTLY DOES IT MEAN TO FOLLOW A PLANT-BASED DIET?

By now it's likely you've heard the term *plant-based diet* or *whole foods plant-based diet*, but what exactly does it mean?

It's not a diet in the traditional sense, and there are no strict guidelines; rather, a plant-based diet puts the emphasis on eating unrefined, minimally processed, nutrient-dense whole foods derived from plants—think whole grains, vegetables, fruit, beans, legumes, nuts, and seeds—while avoiding meat and animal products, like eggs, dairy products, and honey.

The way a plant-based diet is interpreted and followed can vary from person to person. Again, there's a lot of gray area and no real rules here. Ultimately, it's about doing what best meets your needs and feels right and healthiest for *you*. For some people, the goal is keeping vegetables and whole grains at the center of the bowl at all times, while simply reducing or limiting the amount of meat and animal products they consume. For others, it can mean eliminating animal products altogether. Strict followers of the diet may also prefer to cut out cooking oils, as they have a low nutritional value. The commonality here is eating a diet primarily focused on plant-derived whole foods and avoiding processed and refined foods.

BUILDING YOUR BEST PLANT-BASED BOWL

The beauty of Buddha bowls is that anything goes! There are no strict rules when it comes to building these one-bowl meals. In fact, I believe they require more of a template and some inspiration than a recipe that's set in stone. It's a meal that's so incredibly versatile and highly adaptable, which means that swapping different ingredients in or out of a recipe is easy. Get the foundation for building a Buddha bowl down and you'll see endless possibilities for how easy it is to make them your own.

When building Buddha bowls, I like to break the meal down into four basic components: the base, a protein, vegetables, and a sauce or dressing.

Start with a Base

To get started, each Buddha bowl begins with a base, which can take a variety of forms. Rice, whole grains, and noodles are common choices, and in some cases, there's crossover between the base and other components of the bowl. For instance, maybe the bowl starts with a foundation of beans or lentils, which happen to also be the protein source. In other cases, a mix of vegetables serve as the base and the topping.

Always Add a Plant-Based Protein

Adding a wholesome source of plant-based protein is key to creating a bowl with substance that promises to fill you up. It doesn't matter whether you're making a Buddha bowl for breakfast, lunch, or dinner, protein is a must. Soy-based tofu and tempeh are two popular plant-based protein choices, in addition to beans and lentils. Nuts and seeds, particularly pumpkin seeds and hemp seeds, are high in protein, and don't forget vegetables like spinach, broccoli, asparagus, and Brussels sprouts, which all offer a modest amount as well.

Pile on the Vegetables

Vegetables—whether raw, steamed, sautéed, roasted, grilled, or pickled—are the heart and soul of any Buddha bowl. Expect fresh produce to make up about half (and in some cases much more!) of the bowl. This is where I prefer to stick with what's fresh and in season, because not only does it taste a lot better, but seasonal produce is much easier to buy locally and is typically less expensive.

When loading your bowl with vegetables, variety is the name of the game. It makes for a more interesting bowl with a variety of tastes and textures, as well as a variety of nutrients.

Top It Off with a Sauce (and Some Extras!)

Every Buddha bowl needs a drizzle of sauce or dressing, or in some cases even a rich and savory broth to finish it off. Sauce is the final component that takes a bowl from good to great by adding another layer of flavor to tie all the ingredients together. The extras—which can be anything from a shower of toasted nuts, a crunchy seed sprinkle, a pile of quick-pickled vegetables, or even some fresh herbs—play a similar role and add extra flavor and more texture to the bowl.

Sauces and extras are essential to making a delectable bowl, which is why I devoted an entire chapter to them. In chapter 1 you'll find 11 basic sauces, many with variations to give you a total of 28 different sauces to choose from. While most of my Buddha bowl recipes include a suggested sauce, go ahead and swap in any sauce that suits your taste.

Get a head start!

Planning ahead and meal prep are a smart cook's best friends. Get a jump on the week ahead by cooking up a pot of grains and lentils, roast a couple trays of vegetables, sauté some leafy greens, chop up fresh produce, and stir together a sauce or two, then turn them into Buddha bowls throughout the week. Not only does it make mealtimes a total breeze, but it also makes eating healthy a whole lot easier. That's why I made a point of noting the make-ahead moments in recipes throughout the book.

SAUCES AND EXTRAS FOR
BUDDHA BOWLS

Chimichurri Sauce

Chimichurri is the bright, vibrant sauce that will liven up any bowl. Made with a bunch of herbs, a little bit of garlic, fresh lemon juice, and a splash of tangy vinegar, it's bursting with freshness and big, bold flavor. Try not to get hung up on plucking the individual cilantro and parsley leaves from the stems—there's a much easier and faster way. Instead, use a knife to shear the leaves from the whole bunch in one or two swipes. You'll get some of the tender stems, but that's okay.

Makes about ¾ cup (180 ml)

1 packed (16 g) cup fresh cilantro
    leaves and tender stems
½ packed cup (30 g) fresh parsley
    leaves
1 clove garlic
2 tablespoons (30 ml) freshly
    squeezed lemon juice
1 tablespoon (15 ml) red wine vinegar
½ teaspoon kosher salt
⅓ cup (80 ml) extra virgin olive oil

Note: Store in an airtight container in the refrigerator for up to 4 days.

Add the herbs, garlic, lemon juice, vinegar, and salt to the bowl of a food processor. Pulse several times until the herbs are finely chopped. Scrape down the sides of the bowl. With the motor running, slowly pour in the oil and process until well combined, about 1 minute.

Try It Here!
- Lentil and Delicata Squash Chimichurri Bowls
- Chipotle Sweet Potato and Black Bean Bowls
- Cauliflower-Polenta Bowls with Greens

Avocado Green Goddess Dressing

Traditional herb-packed green goddess dressing gets its lush, creamy texture from a mix of sour cream and mayo, but not here. This version takes a more wholesome approach with ripe avocado at the helm. Be sure to start with an avocado that's quite ripe, if not a little past its prime, since it will blend up a lot easier.

Add the avocado, scallions, herbs, garlic, oil, lemon juice, salt, and pepper to the bowl of a food processor. Blend continuously until smooth and well combined, scraping down the sides of the bowl as necessary. With the food processor running, add the water, 1 tablespoon (15 ml) at a time, until it reaches the desired consistency.

Try It Here!
· Herby Green Goddess Salad Bowls with Crispy Quinoa
· Brown Rice and Broccoli Goddess Bowls

Makes about ¾ cup (180 ml)

1 medium ripe avocado, peeled
    and pitted
2 scallions
3 tablespoons (7.5 g) packed
    fresh basil
3 tablespoons (7.5 g) packed
    fresh parsley
1 clove garlic
2 tablespoons (30 ml) avocado
    or extra virgin olive oil
Juice from 1 lemon
½ teaspoon kosher salt
¼ teaspoon freshly ground
    black pepper
5 tablespoons (75 ml) water

**Note: Store in an airtight
container in the refrigerator
for up to 3 days.**

Avocado Sauce

If you love adding avocado to your bowl, you're going to want to give this sauce a try. Combined with a squeeze of lemon or lime, a splash of water, and garlic, creamy, ripe avocado is blitzed into a super smooth, pourable bright green sauce.

Makes about 1 cup (240 ml)

1 medium ripe avocado, peeled
   and pitted
½ cup (120 ml) water, plus more
   as needed
Juice from 1 lemon or lime
1 clove garlic
¼ teaspoon kosher salt
¼ teaspoon freshly ground
   black pepper

Note: Store in an airtight container in the refrigerator for up to 3 days.

Place the ingredients in the bowl of a food processor or blender. Process until well combined and smooth, about 1 minute. Thin with additional water, as desired, 1 tablespoon (15 ml) at a time.

VARIATIONS:
Start with the basic recipe above, and add or omit ingredients as noted below.
• **Herbed Avocado Sauce:** Add ¼ cup (10 to 15 g) loosely packed fresh herbs (cilantro, basil, mint, dill).

Try It Here!
· Cauliflower Rice and Black Bean Burrito Bowls
· Summer Farro Bowls
· Summer Bean Bowls

Creamy Cashew Sauce

If you're looking for a mild-mannered and seriously versatile sauce to drizzle over the top of just about any bowl, cashew sauce totally fits the bill. Soaking the cashews for several hours before blending gives them ample time to soften up and get transformed into a super creamy sauce that can be partnered with just about any ingredients. And with a few extra additions, you can use this sauce as the base for a plant-based Caesar dressing, creamy herb sauce, or smoky red pepper sauce.

1 Place the cashews in a jar or bowl, cover with water, and soak for at least 3 hours. Drain.

2 Place the drained cashews, ⅓ cup (80 ml) water, lemon juice, olive oil, garlic, and salt in a food processor or blender. Process until smooth. Thin with more water, a spoonful at a time, as desired.

VARIATIONS:

Start with the basic recipe above and add or omit ingredients as noted below.

- **Cashew Caesar Dressing:** Add zest and juice of 1 lemon, 2 tablespoons (10 g) nutritional yeast, 1 additional tablespoon (15 ml) olive oil, 1 teaspoon Dijon mustard, ½ teaspoon soy sauce, and ¼ teaspoon freshly ground black pepper.
- **Cashew–Roasted Red Pepper Sauce:** Add one 8-ounce (224 g) jar roasted red peppers (drained), 1 additional tablespoon (15 ml) lemon juice, 1 additional tablespoon (15 ml) olive oil, and 1 teaspoon paprika.
- **Creamy Herb Sauce:** Add ¼ cup (4 to 15 g) cilantro, dill, parsley, tarragon, basil leaves, or a combo.

Makes about 1 cup (240 ml)

½ cup (75 g) raw cashews
⅓ cup (80 ml) water, plus more for soaking
Juice from ½ lemon
1 tablespoon (15 ml) extra virgin olive oil
1 small clove garlic
1 teaspoon kosher salt

Note: Store in an airtight container in the refrigerator for up to 4 days.

Try It Here!
- Wild Mushroom and Cauliflower Breakfast Bowls
- Kale and Brussels Caesar Bowls
- Smoky Marinated Lentil Bowls with Roasted Poblanos
- Winter Abundance Bowls

Savory & Sweet Seed Sprinkles

My favorite way to round out any dish is with something crunchy. By far the hardest part of making these sweet and savory seed mixtures is letting them cool completely without pinching a few bites from the baking sheet. I like to shop the bulk bins for the ingredients, so as not to have too many leftovers.

SAVORY Makes 1 scant cup (145 g)

1 teaspoon extra virgin olive oil
¼ cup (35 g) raw pumpkin seeds
¼ cup (35 g) raw sunflower seeds
¼ cup (30 g) raw sliced almonds
2 tablespoons (18 g) raw sesame
   seeds (regular, black, or a mix)
1 tablespoon (8 g) any mix of
   fennel seed, cumin seed, and
   caraway seed
¼ teaspoon kosher salt
¼ teaspoon garlic powder
1 tablespoon (15 ml) pure maple syrup

1 Heat the oil in a large skillet over medium-low heat. Add the nuts and seeds, sprinkle with the salt and garlic powder, and cook, stirring regularly, until fragrant and lightly browned, 8 to 10 minutes. Remove from the heat and stir in the maple syrup.

2 Transfer to a parchment-lined baking sheet, spread in an even layer, and let cool completely.

Try It Here!
- Crispy Kale and Tahini Soba Noodle Bowls
- Roasted Beet Hummus Bowls

SWEET Makes 1½ cups (225 g)

¼ cup (35 g) chopped raw cashews
¼ cup (35 g) raw pumpkin seeds
¼ cup (35 g) raw sunflower seeds
¼ cup (20 g) unsweetened shredded
   coconut
2 tablespoons (18 g) raw sesame
   seeds (regular, black, or a mix)
1 tablespoon (12 g) flaxseeds
¼ cup (35 g) chopped banana chips
2 tablespoons (16 g) cacao nibs

1 Place the cashews, pumpkin seeds, sunflower seeds, coconut, sesame seeds, and flaxseeds in a medium skillet. Toast over medium-low heat, stirring regularly, until fragrant and lightly browned, about 10 minutes.

2 Spread in an even layer on a rimmed baking sheet to cool completely. Stir in the banana chips and cacao nibs.

Try It Here!
- Leftover Brown Rice Breakfast Bowls
- Springtime Cashew Yogurt Bowls
- PB&J Nice Cream Bowls

Note: Store in an airtight container for up to 1 month.

Creamy Hummus

If you've never made your own hummus, try it! I think you'll be surprised at how few ingredients it requires, how unbelievably simple it is to pull off, and, most off all, just how creamy and luscious it is. I've found that one of the most important factors in making a seriously creamy batch of hummus is blending it in the food processor for a little longer than you think is necessary. About 5 minutes is my sweet spot. The recipe includes a few tablespoons of water, though if you prefer your hummus with a slightly thinner consistency, go ahead and add a little more.

Place all the ingredients in the bowl of a food processor fitted with the blade attachment. Process until smooth and creamy, scraping down the sides as necessary, about 5 minutes total. For a thinner consistency, add more water, 1 tablespoon (15 ml) at a time, while the machine is running.

Try It Here!
· Mushroom Shawarma Bowls
· Smoky Brussels Sprout Bowls
· Fattoush Salad Bowls with Bulgur and Hummus

Makes 1½ cups (360 g)

1½ cups (360 g) or 1 (15-ounce [420 g]) can chickpeas, drained and rinsed
¼ cup (60 g) tahini
1 clove garlic
3 tablespoons (45 ml) water, plus more as needed
2 tablespoons (30 ml) extra virgin olive oil
2 tablespoons (30 ml) lemon juice
1 teaspoon kosher salt

Note: Store in an airtight container in the refrigerator for up to 5 days.

Lemon Dressing

Meet the simple, tangy dressing you can use on just about anything. It starts with a couple lemons and a little bit of Dijon mustard or miso paste, which holds it together and adds just a hint of creaminess. Blend in some fresh basil for a sweet, herbal twist; use capers for a pop of briny flavor; or mix in even more miso paste for a super savory flavor and creamy texture.

Makes about ¾ cup (180 ml)

½ cup (120 ml) freshly squeezed
   lemon juice (from 2 or 3 lemons)
¼ cup (60 ml) extra virgin olive oil
1 small clove garlic, grated
1 teaspoon Dijon mustard or
   white miso paste
¼ teaspoon freshly ground
   black pepper

**Note: Store in an airtight
container in the refrigerator
for up to 5 days.**

Place all the ingredients in a lidded jar and shake until emulsified.

VARIATIONS:
Start with the basic recipe above, and add or omit ingredients as noted below.
- **Lemon Basil Dressing:** Add ¼ cup (15 g) fresh basil leaves and prepare the dressing in a food processor, blending until the leaves are totally broken down.
- **Lemon-Caper Dressing:** Add 1 teaspoon Dijon mustard, ½ teaspoon whole-grain mustard, 2 tablespoons (16 g) drained and smashed capers, and 1 teaspoon caper brine.
- **Lemon-Pepper Miso Dressing:** Increase the white miso paste to 2 tablespoons (30 g) and the black pepper to ½ teaspoon.
- **Sumac Lemon Dressing:** Add 1 tablespoon (6 g) ground sumac and 1 teaspoon agave nectar.

Try It Here!
- Morning Greens Bowls
- Bittersweet Butternut Squash and Radicchio Bowls
- Mediterranean Farro Bowls
- Spring Abundance Bowls
- Lentil Niçoise Bowls
- Sicilian Cauliflower Bowls with Kidney Beans and Orzo
- Fattoush Salad Bowls with Bulgur and Hummus

Any Greens Pesto Sauce

This makes a pesto sauce just the way I like it: heavy on the goodies and light on the oil. It's packed with plenty of greens and tiny bits of nuts or seeds, a bright flavor, and not too much oil. The most wonderful thing about pesto is that you can make it with any kind of herbs or leafy greens you have handy. And the same goes for the nuts or seeds. When using herbs like parsley or cilantro, there's no need to pluck the leaves from the stems (how tedious!). Instead, use a knife to shear the leaves from the whole bunch in one or two swipes. You'll get some of the tender stems, but that's okay.

Add the herbs, nuts, nutritional yeast, lemon juice, miso paste, garlic, and salt to the bowl of a food processor or blender. Pulse several times until finely chopped. With the machine running, gradually pour in the olive oil and process until well combined. Thin with more oil, a spoonful at a time, if desired.

SUGGESTED PESTO COMBINATIONS:
- Basil + toasted walnuts
- Kale + toasted almonds
- Arugula + toasted cashews
- Cilantro + toasted pumpkin seeds

Try It Here!
- Kale Pesto Soba Noodle Bowls
- Farmers' Market Bowls
- Orzo Bowls with Arugula Pesto

Makes about ½ cup (120 ml)

2 loosely packed cups (32 to 120 g) herbs or greens

2 tablespoons (18 g) toasted nuts or seeds

2 tablespoons (10 g) nutritional yeast

2 tablespoons (30 ml) freshly squeezed lemon juice

1 teaspoon miso paste, preferably white or yellow

1 clove garlic

¼ teaspoon kosher salt

¼ cup (60 ml) extra virgin olive oil

Note: Store in an airtight container in the refrigerator for up to 5 days.

Miso-Ginger Sauce

This is the sauce I turn to anytime I'm craving the creaminess of cashew sauce but want something with a richer, more punchy flavor. It starts off by soaking raw cashews, just as you would for basic cashew sauce, but includes ultra-savory miso paste, nutty sesame oil, and plenty of fresh ginger for a little kick. I recommend using white miso paste, which has a mellow taste with a hint of sweetness, though yellow or even richer-tasting red miso paste will also work.

Makes about ¾ cup (180 ml)

⅓ cup (95 g) raw unsalted cashews,
    soaked overnight and drained
¼ cup (60 ml) rice vinegar
3 tablespoons (45 ml) water, plus
    more as needed
3 tablespoons (45 g) miso paste
1-inch (2.5 cm) piece fresh ginger,
    peeled and roughly chopped
1 teaspoon toasted sesame oil
1 teaspoon pure maple syrup
1 clove garlic
¼ teaspoon freshly ground
    black pepper

Note: Store in an airtight container in the refrigerator for up to 4 days.

Place all the ingredients in the bowl of a food processor fitted with the blade attachment or a blender. Process until the sauce is smooth, 2 to 3 minutes. Thin with additional water, as desired.

Try It Here!
- Grilled Brassica Bowls
- Tempeh Teriyaki Rice Bowls
- Miso Noodle Bowls with Tempeh Crumbles

Peanut Sauce

Everyone needs a respectable peanut sauce in their roster, and this is the one I've been coming back to for years. It's rich, creamy, and nutty with a little bit of tang, and it's quick and easy to stir together at a moment's notice with just a handful of basic ingredients. It's wonderful as is, but if you're looking for something with some spice, try adding a spoonful or two of sriracha, or consider canned coconut milk for even more creamy richness.

Place all the ingredients in a medium bowl. Whisk until fully combined. Thin with additional water, 1 tablespoon (15 ml) at a time, as desired.

VARIATIONS:
Start with the basic recipe above, and add or omit ingredients as noted below.
• **Spicy Peanut Sauce:** Add 1 to 2 tablespoons (15 to 30 ml) sriracha.
• **Satay Peanut Sauce:** Omit the water, sesame oil, and ginger; add ½ cup (120 ml) unsweetened coconut milk and heat the sauce in a small saucepan, stirring regularly, until smooth and thin.

Try It Here!
· Roasted Vegetable and Kohlrabi Noodle Bowls with Peanut Sauce
· Summer Roll Noodle Bowls
· Satay Noodle Bowls
· Stir-Fried Celery Bowls with Soba Noodles and Spicy Peanut Sauce

Makes about 1 cup (240 ml)

½ cup (120 g) natural creamy peanut butter
3 tablespoons (45 ml) soy sauce or tamari
3 tablespoons (45 ml) rice vinegar or freshly squeezed lime juice
3 tablespoons (45 ml) water, plus more as needed
2 teaspoons pure maple syrup
1 teaspoon toasted sesame oil
1 tablespoon (8 g) finely grated fresh ginger
1 clove garlic, grated

Note: Store in an airtight container in the refrigerator for up to 4 days.

Tahini Sauce

If I could pick just one sauce to drizzle over my bowls, it would be this tahini sauce, every single time. Below is the recipe for my basic tahini sauce, which is kissed with a little bit of lemon and garlic, followed by a few ideas for flavorful variations, using herbs, even more lemon, or miso paste. The sauce is simple enough to whisk together in a bowl, but if you're making herby green tahini, I suggest using a food processor to pulverize the herbs. As you mix the sauce, it will look curdled at first, but it comes together for a smooth, creamy sauce that's on the thinner side, so it's perfect for drizzling.

Makes about 1 cup (240 ml)

½ cup (120 g) tahini
⅓ cup (80 ml) water
¼ cup (60 ml) freshly squeezed
   lemon juice
1 clove garlic, minced
½ teaspoon kosher salt
¼ teaspoon freshly ground
   black pepper

Note: Store in an airtight container in the refrigerator for up to 5 days.

Place all the ingredients in a medium bowl and whisk until well combined. Thin with additional water or lemon juice, as desired.

VARIATIONS:
Start with the basic recipe above, and add or omit ingredients as noted below.
• **Green Tahini Sauce:** Add ½ cup mixed fresh herbs (like parsley, cilantro, dill, mint, basil); prepare the sauce using a food processor and blend until the herbs are completely blended.
• **Lemon Tahini Sauce:** Increase the lemon juice to ⅓ cup (80 ml) and reduce the water to 3 tablespoons (45 ml).
• **Miso Tahini Sauce:** Add 1 tablespoon (15 ml) soy sauce or tamari and 2 teaspoons miso paste, and swap the lemon juice for rice vinegar.

Try It Here!
• Harissa Carrot Bowls
• Spicy Sesame Tofu and Broccoli Bowls
• Turmeric Quinoa Bowls
• BBQ Tofu Quinoa Bowls
• Crunchy Collard Bowls
• Autumn Harvest Bowls
• Crispy Kale and Tahini Soba Noodle Bowls
• Eggplant and Mushroom Soba Noodle Bowls

Whipped Tahini

Upon first glance, there's a chance you might mistake whipped tahini for hummus. The two look a lot alike, and whipped tahini even has an airy, silky smooth, creamy texture that's reminiscent of hummus. But you won't find any chickpeas here. Just tahini, a squeeze of lemon, a hint of garlic, and a splash of cold water. I recommend starting with a good-quality jar of tahini (my favorites are Soom and Seed + Mill). It makes for a much better spread.

Place the tahini, garlic, salt, and lemon juice in a food processor and pulse to combine. With the machine running, slowly pour in the cold water. Process until smooth, light, and aerated, pausing to scrape down the sides and bottom of the bowl partway through, 3 to 4 minutes total. Add more water as needed until it reaches the desired consistency.

Makes ¾ cup (180 ml)

½ cup (120 g) tahini
1 small clove garlic
½ teaspoon kosher salt
2 tablespoons (30 ml) freshly
   squeezed lemon juice
⅓ cup (80 ml) cold water, plus more
   as needed

Try It Here!
· Roasted Ratatouille Bowls
· Harissa Green Bean Bowls with Whipped Tahini

Note: Store in an airtight container in the refrigerator for up to 3 days.

Hazelnut Dukkah

Dukkah is an Egyptian spice blend typically made with toasted and crushed nuts and seeds that's warm and earthy, and best of all has a really great crunch. There are plenty of premade options but I love making my own to tailor it just the way I like it: heavy on the hazelnuts and sesame seeds, with a hint of salt. It's a natural topping you can use to finish off almost any bowl. You can also use it as a coating for tofu, tossed with a pan of roasted vegetables, or mixed with sautéed greens.

Makes about 1 cup (145 g)

⅓ cup (50 g) raw hazelnuts
¼ cup (35 g) raw pistachios
3 tablespoons (28 g) raw
   sesame seeds
2 tablespoons (16 g) coriander seeds
1 tablespoon (8 g) cumin seeds
½ teaspoon kosher salt
¼ teaspoon freshly ground
   black pepper

Note: Store in an airtight container for up to 1 month.

1 Toast the hazelnuts and pistachios in a large skillet over medium-low heat, stirring regularly, until lightly golden, about 5 minutes. Add the sesame, coriander, and cumin seeds. Continue to toast, stirring regularly, until fragrant and the sesame seeds are lightly browned, about 3 minutes more. Transfer to a baking sheet to cool completely.

2 Add the toasted nuts and seeds, salt, and pepper to a food processor fitted with the blade attachment. Pulse several times until a coarse mixture forms.

Try It Here!
· Smoky Brussels Sprout Bowls
· Kale Pesto Soba Noodle Bowls

Quick-Pickled Vegetables

Quick-pickled vegetables just might be the ultimate bowl topper. They have a tangy acidity, often accompanied with at least a little bit of crunch, that livens up any other ingredients they're partnered with. If you've never quick-pickled vegetables before, I assure you it's easier than it might sound and doesn't take a long time. You'll want to stick with crisp, firm vegetables, like cabbage, radishes, fennel, carrots, onion, and cucumbers, which should be thinly sliced or shredded. Then it's a matter of boiling equal parts vinegar and water, along with a pinch of salt. You'll pour the hot liquid over the vegetables and let them soak. More time is always better to get more flavor, but as little as 10 minutes will get the job done. This basic recipe calls for distilled white vinegar, but you can also try using apple cider vinegar or rice vinegar to change it up.

1 Finely slice, shred, or grate the vegetable. Place in a medium to large heatproof bowl.

2 Place the vinegar, water, and salt in a small saucepan. Bring to a boil over medium-high heat, stirring regularly, until the salt is dissolved. Pour the liquid over the vegetables and set aside for at least 10 minutes and up to 1 hour. Drain and discard the liquid.

Yield varies

Up to 1 pound (455 g) fresh
    vegetables, such as red onion,
    red cabbage, radishes, fennel,
    cucumber, and/or carrots
1 cup (240 ml) distilled white vinegar
1 cup (240 ml) water
1 teaspoon kosher salt

**Note: Store in the refrigerator
for up to 5 days.**

Try It Here!
- Turmeric Quinoa Bowls
- BBQ Tofu Quinoa Bowls
- Harissa Green Bean Bowls with Whipped Tahini
- Cuban-Style Black Bean Bowls
- Spiced Red Lentil Bowls
- Crispy Kale and Tahini Soba Noodle Bowls
- Mushroom Shawarma Bowls
- Roasted Beet Hummus Bowls

BREAKFAST
BOWLS

Turmeric and Coconut Overnight Oat Bowls

Mixing together a bowl of overnight oats is one of the best gifts you can give your future self. Prep it in the evening and by morning you have a wholesome, super creamy bowl of oats waiting for you to dig in. No heating necessary. Overnight oats are meant to be eaten chilled or at room temperature. Any type of nondairy milk will work, though I particularly love oat or cashew milk for the creaminess.

Serves 4 to 6

2 cups (160 g) old-fashioned
    rolled oats
2 tablespoons (16 g) chia seeds
2 tablespoons (14 g) ground flaxseed
1 teaspoon ground turmeric
¼ teaspoon ground ginger
¼ teaspoon ground cinnamon
⅛ teaspoon ground cardamom
2½ cups (600 ml) unsweetened
    nondairy milk
1 cup (240 g) unsweetened coconut
    yogurt
2 tablespoons (30 ml) pure maple
    syrup
1 teaspoon vanilla extract
⅛ teaspoon kosher salt

To serve
Sliced banana
Fresh raspberries
Unsweetened toasted coconut flakes

1 Combine the ingredients in a large bowl and mix until well combined. Cover and refrigerate overnight.

2 To serve, stir the oats once more. Divide among four to six bowls and top with sliced banana, fresh raspberries, and unsweetened toasted coconut flakes.

Vegetable and Tofu Scramble Bowls

Here's your ticket to a veggie-filled, protein-rich breakfast. To me, tofu's number one attribute is its chameleon-like ability to pick up the flavors of any other ingredients it's partnered with. In this savory breakfast bowl, it's cooked alongside sweet onions and bell pepper, mushrooms and spinach, and flavored with umami-rich soy sauce and a sprinkle of nutritional yeast.

1 Place the quinoa, 1¾ cups (420 ml) of the water, and a pinch of salt in a medium saucepan. Bring to a boil over medium-high heat, reduce the heat to low, cover, and cook until tender, about 12 minutes. Remove from the heat and keep covered for 5 minutes. Fluff the quinoa with a fork.

2 Meanwhile, heat the remaining 2 tablespoons (30 ml) water in a large skillet over medium-high heat. Add the spinach, and cook, tossing regularly until wilted, 1 to 2 minutes. Transfer to a bowl; set aside.

3 Heat the oil in the same skillet over medium-high heat until shimmering. Add the onion, bell pepper, mushrooms, and garlic and season with ½ teaspoon kosher salt and a few grinds of black pepper. Cook, stirring occasionally, until the mushrooms release their liquid and it's been cooked off, 8 to 10 minutes. Meanwhile, place the tofu in a medium bowl and crumble into small curds with your fingers.

4 Add the tofu to the skillet, season with ½ teaspoon kosher salt and a few grinds of black pepper, and cook for about 2 minutes. Stir in the carrot, nutritional yeast, soy sauce, and turmeric until well combined, and cook for 2 more minutes.

5 To serve, divide the quinoa, tofu scramble, and spinach among four bowls. Drizzle with tahini.

Serves 4

1 cup (175 g) uncooked quinoa, rinsed
1¾ cups (420 ml) plus 2 tablespoons (30 ml) water, divided
Kosher salt and freshly ground black pepper
4 large handfuls baby spinach
1 tablespoon (15 ml) avocado or extra virgin olive oil
1 small yellow onion, diced
1 medium red bell pepper, cored, seeded, and diced
8 ounces (225 g) cremini mushrooms, thinly sliced
2 cloves garlic, minced
14 ounces (392 g) extra-firm tofu, pressed and drained
½ cup (55 g) shredded carrot
2 tablespoons (10 g) nutritional yeast
1 tablespoon (15 ml) soy sauce or tamari
1 teaspoon ground turmeric
Tahini, for topping

Get a head start! | The quinoa, spinach, and tofu mixture can all be made in advance and reheated before serving.

Tropical Green Smoothie Bowls

Unlike the smoothies you're used to drinking, this version is extra thick, which makes it perfect for piling on the toppings. Not only does avocado make for an even creamier smoothie, but it also adds some good fat to make your bowl more filling. You'll want to pop a couple of bowls in the freezer before blending the smoothie (though if you think about it, go ahead and do this the night before—you'll love the chill it brings to breakfast).

Serves 2

2 cups (480 ml) coconut water
1 cup (240 ml) unsweetened
     nondairy milk
1½ packed cups (45 g) baby spinach
1½ cups (245 g) frozen pineapple
     chunks
1½ cups (255 g) frozen mango chunks
1 medium banana, chopped and frozen
½ ripe avocado
1 pitted date
2 tablespoons (14 g) flaxseed meal
2 tablespoons (16 g) hemp seeds

To serve
Granola
Unsweetened toasted coconut flakes
Hemp seeds

1 Place two bowls in the freezer while you prepare the smoothie. (You can even freeze them the night before.)

2 Add all ingredients to a blender and blend on high speed until smooth and creamy, using the tamper as necessary. Divide between two bowls and top with granola, unsweetened coconut flakes, and additional hemp seeds.

Breakfast Burrito Bowls

If you can't find already prepared sweet potato rice in the produce section, it's easy to make your own. Start with 1 pound (455 g) of sweet potato noodles or peel and spiralize a 1-pound (455 g) sweet potato, then chop the noodles into rice-size pieces. You could use a box grater in a pinch, though the sweet potato "grains" will be thinner, so you want to reduce the cook time by a couple of minutes and the result won't have the same texture and bite.

1 Heat 1 tablespoon (15 ml) of the oil in a large nonstick skillet over medium heat until shimmering. Add the sweet potato rice, season with salt and pepper, and cook, stirring occasionally, until tender and lightly browned, 8 to 10 minutes.

2 Meanwhile, place the tofu in a medium bowl and break into small curds with your fingers. Heat the remaining 1 tablespoon (15 ml) oil in a separate large skillet over medium-high heat until shimmering. Add the onion, bell pepper, and garlic, and cook, stirring occasionally, until softened, about 5 minutes. Add the tofu, season with salt and pepper, and cook for about 2 minutes. Stir in the nutritional yeast, cumin, and paprika, and continue cooking for 4 minutes longer.

3 To serve, divide the sweet potato rice and scrambled tofu among four bowls. Top with the black beans, avocado, sliced scallions, and salsa.

Serves 4

2 tablespoons (30 ml) avocado or extra virgin olive oil, divided
1 pound (455 g) sweet potato rice
Kosher salt and freshly ground black pepper
14 ounces (392 g) extra-firm tofu, pressed and drained
1 small yellow onion, diced
1 medium bell pepper, cored, seeded, and diced
2 cloves garlic, minced
3 tablespoons (15 g) nutritional yeast
2 teaspoons ground cumin
1 teaspoon sweet paprika
1½ cups (360 g) or 1 (15-ounce [420 g]) can black beans, drained and rinsed
1 avocado, peeled, pitted, and quartered
2 scallions, green part only, thinly sliced
½ cup (120 ml) salsa

Get a head start! | The tofu can be cooked a day in advance and reheated before serving.

Maple-Tahini Multigrain Porridge Bowls

I'll take just about any excuse to work tahini into my breakfast, especially porridge. It has a nutty, slightly bitter flavor, and I love the way it plays with the warmth of the toasted grains and balances the sweetness of the maple. You'll mix a few spoonfuls of tahini into the porridge, and I recommend drizzling more over the top of the bowl for serving.

Serves 4

⅓ cup (35 g) steel-cut oats
⅓ cup (65 g) pearl barley
⅓ cup (60 g) uncooked quinoa, rinsed
2 cups (480 ml) water
Kosher salt
1½ cups (360 ml) unsweetened non-dairy milk, plus more for serving, if desired
3 tablespoons (45 g) tahini, plus more for serving
3 tablespoons (45 ml) pure maple syrup
2 tablespoons (14 g) flaxseed meal
2 Bosc pears, cored and chopped
¼ cup (35 g) chopped toasted walnuts

1 Toast the oats, barley, and quinoa in a large, dry saucepan over medium heat, shaking occasionally, until fragrant and lightly browned, about 5 minutes. Pour in the water and a pinch of salt. The water will sputter but will settle down quickly. Bring to a boil over medium-high heat, then reduce the heat to low and simmer, uncovered, stirring occasionally, until most but not all of the water is absorbed, about 10 minutes. Pour in the milk and continue cooking, stirring occasionally and scraping the bottom and corners of the pot, until the grains are tender and creamy, about 15 minutes. Remove from the heat and stir in the tahini, maple syrup, and flaxseed meal.

2 To serve, divide the porridge among four bowls and add more milk, if desired. Top with the chopped pear and walnuts, and drizzle with tahini.

Get a head start! | The porridge can be made a day in advance and reheated before serving. Thin with additional milk when reheating, if desired, and wait until serving to add the toppings.

Morning Glory Barley Bowls

Have you ever had a morning glory muffin? Scented with warm cinnamon and ginger and stuffed with a mix of shredded carrot, apple, toasted walnuts, and coconut, they're quick to remind me of fall, though definitely worth eating all year long. And these just-sweet-enough muffins are also the inspiration for this creamy, wholesome breakfast bowl. It packs in everything there is to love about the classic muffin and tastes best when you get a little bit of everything in one bite, so it's creamy, sweet, bitter, nutty, chewy, and crunchy.

1 Place the barley, water, milk, and a pinch of salt in a large saucepan. Bring to a boil over medium-high heat, then reduce the heat to low, partially cover, and simmer, stirring occasionally, until tender and most but not all of the liquid has been absorbed, 25 to 30 minutes. Remove from the heat and stir in the carrot, orange zest and juice, maple syrup, cinnamon, and ginger. Cover with the lid and steam for 5 minutes.

2 To serve, divide the barley among four bowls. Finish with an extra splash of milk, if desired, and top with the chopped apple, walnuts, pumpkin seeds, and toasted coconut flakes.

Serves 4

1 cup (200 g) pearl barley
3 cups (720 ml) water
1½ cups (360 ml) unsweetened cashew or almond milk, plus more for serving, if desired
Kosher salt
1 cup (110 g) grated carrot
Finely grated zest and juice from 1 navel orange
3 tablespoons (45 ml) pure maple syrup
¾ teaspoon ground cinnamon
½ teaspoon ground ginger
1 apple, cored and chopped
½ cup (70 g) chopped toasted walnuts
½ cup (70 g) toasted pumpkin seeds
½ cup (40 g) unsweetened toasted coconut flakes

Get a head start! | The barley can be made in advance and reheated in the morning. Just wait until you're ready to eat to add the toppings so they stay crunchy.

Savory Miso Oat and Lentil Bowls with Charred Scallions

In case you're in need of a reminder, there's a savory side to oats, and it's scrumptious. Here, steel-cut oats are partnered with red lentils to form a complete protein, so you can start your day on the right foot. Green and brown lentils are known for holding their shape during cooking, so be sure to stick with the red variety, which fall apart as they cook down, adding lots of creaminess. For an extra pop of savory flavor, finish off the bowl with a little bit of warm vegetable broth.

1 Bring 4 cups (960 ml) of the water to a boil in a large saucepan. Add the oats and lentils, season with a pinch of salt, reduce the heat to low, cover, and simmer until tender and most of the liquid is absorbed, about 30 minutes, stirring occasionally and scraping the bottom of the pot to prevent the oats from sticking. Remove from the heat, add the miso paste and soy sauce, and stir well until dissolved.

2 Meanwhile, heat the remaining 2 tablespoons (30 ml) water in a large skillet over medium heat. Add the spinach and cook, tossing occasionally, until wilted, about 2 minutes. Transfer to a bowl; set aside.

3 Wipe the skillet clean and heat the oil over medium-high heat until shimmering. Add the scallions, season with a pinch of salt, and cook, tossing occasionally, until lightly charred all over, 4 to 5 minutes.

4 To serve, divide the oat and lentil mixture among four bowls. Top with the spinach, charred scallions, and sliced radish. If desired, for creamier oats, pour the vegetable broth around the edge of the bowls. Garnish with the pumpkin seeds and sesame seeds.

Serves 4

4 cups (960 ml) plus 2 tablespoons (30 ml) water, divided
¾ cup (60 g) steel-cut oats
½ cup (100 g) red lentils
Kosher salt
1 tablespoon (15 g) white miso paste
1 tablespoon (15 ml) soy sauce or tamari
4 packed cups (120 g) baby spinach
1 tablespoon (15 ml) avocado or extra virgin olive oil
1 bunch scallions, ends trimmed and cut into 2-inch (5 cm) pieces
4 radishes, thinly sliced
1 cup (240 ml) low-sodium vegetable broth, warmed (optional)
¼ cup (35 g) toasted pumpkin seeds
1 tablespoon (9 g) black sesame seeds

Get a head start! | The oat and lentil mixture, spinach, and scallions can be cooked in advance. When reheating, you may want to use a splash of water or vegetable broth to loosen the mixture.

Leftover Brown Rice Breakfast Bowls

These simple breakfast bowls will forever change your feelings about leftover rice. And if you're anything like me, you'll intentionally cook extra rice from now on. The recipe calls for two cups of rice, though it's easy to scale up or down depending on the amount you happen to have. Just remember that you'll simmer equal parts rice and nondairy milk, until it's warm, slightly thickened, and creamy.

Serves 4

2 cups (330 g) cooked brown rice
2 cups (480 ml) unsweetened
   nondairy milk
2 tablespoons (30 ml) pure maple
   syrup
½ teaspoon ground cinnamon
¼ teaspoon ground cardamom
1 teaspoon pure vanilla extract
2 cups (240 g) unsweetened
   nondairy yogurt
Mixed berries
¼ cup (35 g) Sweet Seed Sprinkle
   (page 16)

1 Place the rice, milk, maple syrup, cinnamon, and cardamom in a large saucepan. Bring to a boil over medium-high heat, then reduce the heat to low and simmer until thickened and most but not all of the liquid is absorbed, about 10 minutes. Remove from the heat and stir in the vanilla.

2 To serve, divide the rice among four bowls. Top with the yogurt, berries, and Sweet Seed Sprinkle.

Springtime Cashew Yogurt Bowls

There are few combos I love more than tart rhubarb and sweet strawberries. We all know they make a lovely pie or shortcake filling, and they also happen to make a wonderful breakfast addition. Here, the duo is roasted with a hint of maple and a squeeze of lemon. Roasting draws out the fruit's natural sweetness, so even if your berries are just okay, this will transform them into something great. The compote can be served slightly warmed, at room temperature, or chilled.

1 Arrange a rack in the middle of the oven and preheat to 350ºF (180ºC or gas mark 4).

2 Place the rhubarb, strawberries, maple syrup, and lemon zest and juice on a parchment-lined baking sheet and toss well to combine. Bake until the fruit is soft, about 20 minutes, stirring once halfway through. Set aside to cool slightly.

3 Meanwhile, toast the buckwheat in a dry skillet over medium-low heat, stirring occasionally, until fragrant and lightly browned all over, 5 to 8 minutes. Set aside to cool completely.

4 To serve, stir the cardamom into the yogurt until well distributed and divide among four bowls. Top with the strawberry-rhubarb compote, toasted buckwheat, and Sweet Seed Sprinkle.

Serves 4

4 stalks rhubarb, cut into 1-inch (2.5 cm) pieces
1 pound (455 g) strawberries, tops removed and quartered
2 tablespoons (30 ml) pure maple syrup
Zest and juice of 1 lemon
½ cup (100 g) buckwheat
½ teaspoon ground cardamom
4 cups (960 g) unsweetened cashew yogurt
¼ cup (35 g) Sweet Seed Sprinkle (page 16)

Get a head start! | The strawberry-rhubarb compote can be made a day in advance and stored in the refrigerator until ready to serve.

Morning Greens Bowls

This is really an all-day bowl, but I most often find myself eating it in the morning. Loaded with superfoods, like quinoa, sweet potatoes, kale, blueberries, and walnuts, it's the breakfast that, without fail, always makes me feel supercharged and ready to take on the day.

Serves 4

1 bunch Tuscan kale, center ribs removed and leaves chopped
2 tablespoons (30 ml) extra virgin olive oil, divided
Juice from 1 lemon
Kosher salt and freshly ground black pepper
2 medium sweet potatoes, peeled and cut into wedges
¾ cup (140 g) tricolor quinoa, rinsed
⅓ cup (65 g) brown lentils, rinsed
1¾ cups (420 ml) water
2 avocados, peeled, pitted, and halved
1 cup (150 g) blueberries
¼ cup (35 g) chopped toasted walnuts
¼ cup (35 g) toasted unsalted pumpkin seeds
1 recipe Lemon Dressing (page 18)

1 Preheat the oven to 425ºF (220ºC or gas mark 7).

2 Place the kale in a large bowl, drizzle with 1 tablespoon (15 ml) of the oil, the lemon juice, and a pinch of salt. Massage the kale so it's well coated. Set aside.

3 Place the sweet potatoes on a rimmed baking sheet, drizzle with the remaining 1 tablespoon (15 ml) oil, sprinkle with salt and a few grinds of black pepper, and toss together. Spread in a single layer and roast until tender and browned, tossing once halfway through, about 30 minutes total.

4 Place the quinoa, lentils, water, and a pinch of salt in a medium saucepan. Bring to a boil over medium-high heat, then reduce the heat to low, cover, and cook until tender, about 15 minutes. Remove from the heat and keep covered for 5 minutes. Fluff with a fork.

5 To serve, divide the kale and quinoa mixture among four bowls. Top with the roasted sweet potato wedges, avocado, blueberries, walnuts, and pumpkin seeds. Drizzle with the dressing.

Get a head start! | The kale can be massaged, sweet potatoes roasted, the quinoa mixture cooked, and the dressing made a day in advance. Reheat when you're ready to eat.

Creamy Millet Porridge with Peaches and Pistachios

If oatmeal has been your go-to breakfast cereal until now, I encourage you to give millet a try. Cooked with your choice of nondairy milk, plus coconut milk for richness, millet cooks up into an extra creamy porridge, plus it comes with a long list of nutritional benefits. This gluten-free cereal grain is super high in calcium, packed with protein, and rich in fiber and antioxidants. Talk about a strong start to the day!

Serves 4

2 cups (480 ml) unsweetened nondairy milk, plus more for serving, if desired

1 cup (240 ml) unsweetened canned coconut milk

2 tablespoons (30 ml) pure maple syrup

¼ teaspoon ground cardamom

2 cups (400 g) cooked millet

1 teaspoon pure vanilla extract

2 medium ripe peaches, pitted and sliced

¼ cup (35 g) toasted pistachios

3 tablespoons (15 g) unsweetened toasted coconut flakes

1 Place the milks, maple syrup, and cardamom in a medium saucepan. Stir in the millet and break up any clumps. Bring to a boil over medium-high heat, then reduce the heat to low and simmer until thickened and creamy, about 15 minutes. Remove from the heat and stir in the vanilla.

2 To serve, divide the millet among four bowls and top with additional nondairy milk, if desired. Top with the sliced peaches, toasted pistachios, and toasted coconut flakes.

Wild Mushroom and Cauliflower Breakfast Bowls

Every time I go to this small café in my neighborhood, I *know* I'm going to order the wild mushroom toast. I grab a menu anyway, considering it will be the day I finally order something different. But I just can't do it. Kissed with a hint of umami-rich miso paste and partnered with a pile of peppery watercress, creamy avocado, and tangy red onion, these bowls are how I bring my favorite order to life at home.

1 Heat 2 tablespoons (30 ml) of the oil in a large skillet over medium heat until shimmering. Add the mushrooms, season with a pinch of salt and pepper, and cook, stirring occasionally, until softened, about 10 minutes. Add the miso paste and stir to coat the mushrooms until the miso is mostly dissolved, and cook for 1 minute more. Transfer the mushrooms to a plate and set aside.

2 Heat the remaining 1 tablespoon (15 ml) oil in the same skillet over medium heat. Add the cauliflower rice, season with salt and pepper, and cook, stirring occasionally, until the cauliflower is tender, 3 to 5 minutes. Stir in the edamame and cook for 2 minutes more.

3 To serve, divide the cauliflower rice among four bowls. Top with the watercress, sautéed mushrooms, and avocado. Drizzle with the Creamy Cashew Sauce and finish with a pile of pickled red onion.

Serves 4

3 tablespoons (45 ml) avocado or extra virgin olive oil, divided

1 pound (455 g) mixed mushrooms, such as cremini, shiitake, and oyster, sliced

Kosher salt and freshly ground black pepper

1 tablespoon (15 g) miso paste, preferably white

1 pound (454 g) cauliflower rice, fresh or frozen

1 cup (150 g) shelled edamame, thawed if frozen

1 small bunch watercress, ends trimmed

1 avocado, peeled, pitted, and quartered

1 recipe Creamy Cashew Sauce (page 15)

1 small red onion, thinly sliced and pickled (page 25)

VEGETABLE POWER
BOWLS

Herby Green Goddess Salad Bowls with Crispy Quinoa

This reminds me of a bowl I'd see on the menu at one of those salad places. Thanks to those bright pops of vibrant color and crispy quinoa topping, I'd order it based on looks alone. I prefer to use a mandoline to slice the fennel and radishes to keep them as thin as can be, but a sharp knife also works. If your fennel contains the fronds, which taste similar to dill, go ahead and mix some in with the kale and herbs.

1 Arrange a rack in the middle of the oven and preheat to 350°F (180°C or gas mark 4).

2 Spread the cooked quinoa in an even layer on a rimmed baking sheet. Bake until the quinoa is golden brown and crisp, about 30 minutes, stirring every 10 minutes. Let cool completely.

3 Place the baby kale and herbs in a large bowl and toss to combine.

4 Divide the greens among four bowls. Top with the crispy quinoa, white beans, Persian cucumbers, fennel, watermelon radishes, and regular radishes. Spoon the Avocado Green Goddess Dressing over the top and sprinkle with the chopped almonds.

Get a head start! | The crispy quinoa can be cooked a day in advance. Once completely cooled, store in an airtight container at room temperature.

Serves 4

2 cups (370 g) cooked quinoa
4 ounces (112 g) baby kale
½ packed cup (30 g) fresh basil leaves, coarsely chopped
½ packed cup (30 g) fresh mint leaves, coarsely chopped
1½ cups (360 g) or 1 (15-ounce [420 g]) can white beans, drained and rinsed
2 Persian cucumbers, thinly sliced
1 small fennel bulb, thinly sliced
1 large watermelon radish, thinly sliced
4 radishes, thinly sliced
1 recipe Avocado Green Goddess Dressing (page 13)
½ cup (70 g) chopped toasted almonds

Sesame-Ginger Tempeh and Brown Rice Bowls

I'm a strong believer in using smart shortcuts whenever possible to make mealtimes a little easier and to reduce the amount of dirty dishes. Here, that means whisking together a pantry marinade for the tempeh that gets turned into a creamy sauce to drizzle over the bowls. Be sure to use a bigger pot than you think you need for cooking the broccoli, because partway through you'll toss in the bok choy to steam.

Serves 4

¼ cup (60 ml) soy sauce or tamari
2 tablespoons (30 ml) rice vinegar
2 teaspoons sambal olek
2 teaspoons pure maple syrup
1 tablespoon (8 g) finely grated fresh ginger
2 cloves garlic, grated
8 ounces (225 g) tempeh, cubed
¼ cup (60 g) tahini
2 cups (480 ml) plus 2 tablespoons (30 ml) water, divided
1 cup (165 g) brown rice
Kosher salt
1 tablespoon (15 ml) avocado or extra virgin olive oil
1 small head broccoli, cut into bite-size pieces
4 heads baby bok choy, trimmed and halved lengthwise
Toasted sesame seeds
Red pepper flakes

1 Stir together the soy sauce, rice vinegar, sambal olek, maple syrup, ginger, and garlic in a small bowl. Spoon 3 tablespoons (45 ml) of the sauce into a separate bowl, add the tempeh, stir to coat, and marinate for at least 10 minutes. Whisk the tahini and 2 tablespoons (30 ml) of the water into the remaining sauce; set aside.

2 Meanwhile, add the rice, remaining 2 cups (480 ml) water, and a pinch of salt to a saucepan and bring to a boil over medium-high heat. Reduce the heat to low, cover, and cook until the rice is tender and the liquid is absorbed, about 30 minutes. Remove from the heat, and steam the rice with the lid on for 5 minutes.

3 Meanwhile, heat the oil in a medium skillet over medium-high heat until shimmering. Add the tempeh and cook, stirring occasionally, until golden brown all over, 6 to 8 minutes.

4 Place the broccoli florets in a steamer basket fitted in a large saucepan, add 2 inches (5 cm) of water to the pan, and place over medium heat. Cover and steam until the broccoli is tender, about 5 minutes. With 2 minutes to go, place the bok choy over the broccoli.

5 To serve, stir the sauce together once more. Divide the rice among four bowls and top with the bok choy, broccoli, and tempeh. Drizzle with the sauce and garnish with the sesame seeds and a pinch of red pepper flakes.

Roasted Ratatouille Bowls

Inspired by classic summery ratatouille, this version starts with a couple of baking sheets for an easy twist. All the usual suspects—eggplant, summer squash, bell pepper, tomatoes, and onion—along with some hearty chickpeas are piled on the baking sheets and roasted until lightly charred and tender. Even if you're not working with summer vegetables in their prime (especially tomatoes!), roasting coaxes out an irresistible flavor. You'll round out the bowls with nutty cracked freekeh and plenty of silky smooth whipped tahini.

1 Arrange oven racks to divide the oven into thirds and preheat to 400°F (200°C or gas mark 6).

2 Place the eggplant, squash, bell peppers, tomatoes, onion, chickpeas, and garlic in a large bowl, drizzle with the oil, season with a pinch of salt and a few grinds of black pepper, and toss to coat. Divide the vegetables between two rimmed baking sheets and spread in an even layer. Add two sprigs of the thyme to each baking sheet.

3 Roast until the vegetables are tender and lightly browned, about 40 minutes, stirring and rotating the baking sheets once halfway through. Remove from the oven, drizzle each pan of vegetables with 1 teaspoon of the balsamic vinegar, and toss to combine.

4 Meanwhile, place the freekeh in a medium saucepan and toast over medium heat until fragrant, about 3 minutes. Pour in the water and a pinch of salt and bring to a boil over medium-high heat. Reduce the heat to low, cover, and simmer until tender and the water is absorbed, 20 to 25 minutes. Remove from the heat and steam for 10 minutes. Fluff with a fork.

5 To serve, spread a layer of Whipped Tahini over the bottom of four bowls, then top with the freekeh and vegetables.

Serves 4

1 pound (455 g) eggplant, chopped

12 ounces (340 g) summer squash or zucchini, chopped

2 medium red or yellow bell peppers, cored, seeded, and chopped

2 pints (300 g) grape tomatoes

1 large yellow onion, halved and sliced into ½-inch (1.3 cm)-thick strips

1½ cups (360 g) or 1 (15-ounce [420 g]) can chickpeas, drained and rinsed

6 cloves garlic, peeled and smashed

2 tablespoons (30 ml) extra virgin olive oil

Kosher salt and freshly ground black pepper

4 sprigs fresh thyme

2 teaspoons balsamic vinegar

1 cup (165 g) cracked freekeh

2½ cups (600 ml) water

1 recipe Whipped Tahini (page 23)

Get a head start! | The vegetables and freekeh can be cooked a day in advance, then reheated before serving.

Bittersweet Butternut Squash and Radicchio Bowls

I hate playing favorites, but if I had to choose, this bowl falls into my top three picks in the book. It has such a fun mix of flavors and textures that keep it interesting. A mix of bitter kale and radicchio balances the sweetness of roasted butternut squash and red onion, and offers both soft and crisp vegetables; crunchy nuts and seeds and chewy farro round out the texture profile. If you want to save a little prep time, pick up a package of precut squash from the produce section.

Serves 4

1½ pounds (680 g) butternut squash, peeled, seeded, and cut into ½-inch (1.3 cm) cubes

1 large red onion, roughly chopped

2 tablespoons (30 ml) avocado or extra virgin olive oil

Kosher salt and freshly ground black pepper

1 cup (175 g) farro, rinsed

4 packed cups (280 g) shredded Tuscan kale (about 1 medium bunch)

1 head radicchio, cored and shredded

4 pitted Medjool dates, chopped

1 recipe Lemon-Pepper Miso Dressing (page 18), divided

¼ cup (35 g) chopped toasted hazelnuts

¼ cup (35 g) toasted sunflower seeds

Get a head start! | The butternut squash, onion, and farro can be cooked in advance and reheated, if desired, before serving.

1 Arrange a rack in the middle of the oven and preheat to 425°F (220°C or gas mark 7).

2 Place the cubed squash and chopped red onion on a rimmed baking sheet, drizzle with the oil, and season with a pinch of salt and a few grinds of black pepper. Arrange in a single layer and roast until tender and lightly browned, 25 to 30 minutes, tossing once halfway through.

3 Meanwhile, place the farro and a pinch of salt in a medium saucepan and cover with water by 2 inches (5 cm). Bring to a boil over medium-high heat, then reduce the heat and simmer uncovered until tender and slightly chewy, 10 to 15 minutes for pearled farro or 25 to 30 minutes for semi-pearled farro. Drain the excess water and set aside.

4 Meanwhile, place the kale, radicchio, chopped dates, and ¼ cup (60 ml) of the Lemon-Pepper Miso Dressing in a large bowl and toss to combine.

5 To serve, divide the kale and radicchio mixture among four bowls. Top with the farro, roasted butternut squash and red onions, chopped hazelnuts, and sunflower seeds. Drizzle with additional dressing, as desired.

Harissa Carrot Bowls

Remember that bag of carrots hanging out in your crisper? It's easy to rely on them as a filler vegetable or a fallback when you're out of everything else, but they have so much potential, and I'm going to show you how to make carrots the most delicious star of the meal. A duo of warm, spiced harissa paste and smoky cumin are the most wonderful friends to sweet, earthy carrots. The roasted carrots are balanced with nutty bulgur, leafy greens, sweet and crunchy pomegranate arils, and a bright, savory sauce.

1 Arrange a rack in the middle of the oven and preheat to 425°F (220°C or gas mark 7).

2 Place the carrots on a rimmed baking sheet, add 2 tablespoons (30 ml) of the oil, plus the harissa, cumin, a pinch of kosher salt, and a few grinds of black pepper, and use your hands to toss together. Arrange the carrots in a single layer. Roast until lightly browned and tender, about 20 minutes, tossing once halfway through.

3 Meanwhile, combine the bulgur, water, and a pinch of salt in a medium saucepan. Bring to a boil over medium-high heat, then reduce the heat to low, cover, and simmer until tender and the water is absorbed, about 15 minutes.

4 Heat the remaining 1 tablespoon (15 ml) oil in a Dutch oven until shimmering. Add the chard and cook, tossing occasionally, until just wilted. Add the garlic and beans, season with a pinch of salt, and cook for 1 minute more.

5 To serve, divide the bulgur among four bowls. Top with the rainbow chard and bean mixture and carrots. Drizzle with the Green Tahini Sauce and sprinkle with the pumpkin seeds and pomegranate arils.

Serves 4

2 pounds (1820 g) carrots, peeled and cut on the diagonal into ¼-inch (6 mm)-thick pieces

3 tablespoons (45 ml) avocado or extra virgin olive oil, divided

1 tablespoon (15 g) harissa paste

½ teaspoon ground cumin

Kosher salt and freshly ground black pepper

1 cup (185 g) bulgur wheat

2 cups (480 ml) water

1 large bunch rainbow chard, trimmed and chopped

1 clove garlic, minced

1½ cups (360 g) or 1 (15-ounce [420 g]) can Great Northern beans, drained and rinsed

1 recipe Green Tahini Sauce made with cilantro (page 22)

½ cup (70 g) toasted pumpkin seeds

½ cup (70 g) pomegranate arils

Get a head start! | The carrots can be roasted, the bulgur cooked, and the chard sautéed in advance and reheated before serving.

Chipotle Sweet Potato and Black Bean Bowls

Despite a mix of humble ingredients, like beans, potatoes, and cabbage, these bowls are anything but boring and far from basic. Instead, these simple ingredients are transformed into a protein-packed meal with lots of big, bold flavors. A trio of pantry spices leave roasted sweet potato wedges with a warm, smoky aroma and kick of heat, while a vibrant, herby chimichurri sauce brings the whole thing to life.

Serves 4

3 medium sweet potatoes, peeled and cut into wedges
1½ tablespoons (23 ml) avocado or extra virgin olive oil
2 teaspoons chipotle chili powder
1 teaspoon ground cumin
½ teaspoon garlic powder
Kosher salt and freshly ground black pepper
1 cup (175 g) quinoa, rinsed
1¾ cups (420 ml) water
2 cups (140 g) finely shredded red cabbage
1 recipe Chimichurri Sauce (page 12), divided
2 cups (480 g) black beans, drained and rinsed
1 avocado, peeled, pitted, and quartered
1 lime, cut into wedges

1 Arrange a rack in the middle of the oven and preheat to 425ºF (220ºC or gas mark 7).

2 Place the sweet potatoes on a rimmed baking sheet, drizzle with the oil, and sprinkle with the chili powder, cumin, garlic powder, salt, and a few grinds of black pepper. Roast until tender and lightly browned, about 25 minutes, flipping the potatoes halfway through.

3 Meanwhile, place the quinoa, water, and a pinch of salt in a medium saucepan. Bring to a boil over medium-high heat, reduce the heat to low, cover, and cook until tender, about 12 minutes. Remove from the heat and keep covered for 5 minutes. Fluff the quinoa with a fork.

4 Toss the cabbage with 2 tablespoons (30 ml) of the Chimichurri Sauce.

5 To serve, divide the quinoa and cabbage among four bowls. Top, in separate piles, with the sweet potato, black beans, and avocado. Spoon the remaining Chimichurri Sauce over the top and serve with a lime wedge.

Get a head start! | The sweet potatoes and quinoa can be cooked a day in advance, then reheated before serving.

Crunchy Collard Bowls

If kale and chard are the tough greens you regularly turn to, it's time to give collard greens a chance. They're commonly braised or sautéed, but this is your reminder that they're really wonderful when eaten raw. Here, shredded collard leaves are partnered with red cabbage and tossed with an herby tahini sauce to make a crunchy slaw base for these packed veggie bowls. Even though collards and cabbage are far sturdier than some other leafy vegetables, wait until just before serving to toss them with the tahini sauce so they don't lose their irresistible crunch.

1 Preheat the oven to 425ºF (220ºC or gas mark 7).

2 In a bowl, toss the sweet potatoes with the oil, salt, and pepper, and arrange in an even layer on a rimmed baking sheet. Roast until tender and lightly browned, flipping the potatoes halfway through, about 25 minutes total.

3 Meanwhile, place the split mung beans and a pinch of salt in a small saucepan and cover with water by at least 2 inches (5 cm). Bring to a boil over medium-high, then reduce the heat and simmer until tender, about 20 minutes. Drain the excess water.

4 Place the shredded collard greens, cabbage, sunflower seeds, and hemp seeds in a large bowl and toss with ⅓ cup (80 ml) of the Green Tahini Sauce.

5 To serve, divide the collard mixture among four bowls. Top with the sweet potatoes, mung beans, avocado, radishes, and kraut. Drizzle with the remaining Green Tahini Sauce and sprinkle with additional sunflower and hemp seeds.

Get a head start! | The sweet potatoes can be roasted and the mung beans cooked in advance, then reheated when ready to eat.

Serves 4

2 medium sweet potatoes (about 1½ pounds [680 g]), peeled and cut into wedges

1 tablespoon (15 ml) avocado or extra virgin olive oil

Kosher salt and freshly ground black pepper

¾ cup (130 g) dried split mung beans

1 small bunch collard greens, stems and center ribs removed and leaves shredded

2 packed cups (140 g) finely shredded red cabbage

¼ cup (35 g) unsalted toasted sunflower seeds, plus more for topping

2 tablespoons (18 g) hemp seeds, plus more for topping

1 recipe Green Tahini Sauce (page 22), divided

1 avocado, peeled, pitted, and chopped

1 small bunch radishes, preferably Easter egg radishes, thinly sliced

1 cup (100 g) fermented red cabbage or beet kraut

Kale and Brussels Caesar Bowls

This salad-inspired bowl is both everything you know and love about classic Caesar salad, and the farthest thing from it at the same time. For starters, the plant-based dressing has an ultra-creamy cashew base, then swaps basic romaine for a mix of hearty kale and shredded Brussels sprouts. You'll toss the green base with some dressing to soften the leaves while you prepare the remainder of the bowl.

Serves 4

1 pound (455 g) Brussels sprouts, trimmed and shredded

1 small bunch Tuscan kale, leaves finely shredded

¼ cup (35 g) hemp seeds

1 recipe Cashew Caesar Dressing (page 15), divided

8 ounces (225 g) tempeh

2 tablespoons (30 ml) freshly squeezed lemon juice

½ teaspoon smoked paprika

¼ teaspoon kosher salt

¼ teaspoon freshly ground black pepper

1 tablespoon (15 ml) extra virgin olive oil

1½ cups (360 g) or 1 (15-ounce [420 g]) can cannellini beans, drained and rinsed

¼ cup (35 g) chopped toasted walnuts

1 Place the Brussels sprouts, kale, hemp seeds, and ¾ cup (180 ml) of the Cashew Caesar Dressing in a large bowl and toss to combine. Set aside.

2 Meanwhile, steam the block of tempeh in a medium saucepan fit with a steamer basket for 10 minutes. Pat dry. When cool enough to handle, crumble into small pieces. Whisk together the lemon juice, paprika, salt, and pepper in a medium bowl until smooth. Add the tempeh to the marinade, gently toss to coat, and let it sit for at least 10 minutes.

3 Heat the oil in a large nonstick skillet over medium-high heat. Add the tempeh and cook, stirring often, until lightly browned all over, 5 to 7 minutes.

4 To serve, divide the greens among four bowls. Top with the tempeh, beans, and walnuts and drizzle with the remaining dressing.

Winter Abundance Bowls

Unlike kale and collards where the center ribs and stems are far too tough to eat, chard is a totally different story. Not only are the crisp stems totally edible, but they're also tasty—especially sautéed until tender alongside the chopped leaves. Chioggia beets, also known as candy cane beets for their contrasting red and white rings, are an eye-catching addition to the bowl. If you can't find them, red or golden beets will work nicely and add the same sweet, peppery crunch.

1 Preheat the oven to 400°F (200°C or gas mark 6).

2 Place the rice, lentils, water, and a pinch of salt in a medium saucepan. Bring to a boil over medium-high heat, then reduce the heat to low, cover, and simmer until tender and the water is mostly absorbed, 25 to 30 minutes.

3 Whisk together 1 tablespoon (15 ml) of the oil, the curry paste, salt, and pepper in a large bowl. Slice the squash in half lengthwise. Scoop out the seeds. Slice crosswise into ½-inch (1.3 cm)-thick crescents. Add the squash to the bowl and toss to coat. Arrange in a single layer on a rimmed baking sheet and roast until tender and lightly browned, flipping once halfway through, about 25 minutes total.

4 Meanwhile, heat the remaining 1 tablespoon (15 ml) oil in a large skillet over medium heat. Add the chard leaves and stems and garlic. Cook, tossing occasionally, until wilted, 3 to 5 minutes.

5 To serve, divide the rice and lentils among four bowls. Top with the delicata squash, chard, beets, and pumpkin seeds, and drizzle with the Creamy Herb Sauce.

Serves 4

¾ cup (120 g) brown rice, rinsed

½ cup (100 g) brown lentils, rinsed

2¼ cups (600 ml) water

Kosher salt and freshly ground black pepper, to taste

2 tablespoons (30 ml) avocado or extra virgin olive oil, divided

1½ teaspoons vegan Thai red curry paste

2 medium delicata squash, scrubbed

1 bunch Swiss chard, leaves shredded and stems chopped

1 clove garlic, grated

2 Chioggia beets, peeled and thinly sliced

⅓ cup (90 g) toasted pumpkin seeds

1 recipe Creamy Herb Sauce made with cilantro (page 15)

Farmers' Market Bowls

Let's call this recipe what it really is—a celebration of summer in a bowl. It's all of my favorite seasonal farmers' market finds—juicy, ripe heirloom tomatoes, sweet corn, summer squash, and fragrant herbs—brought together for a fresh, filling meal. While I recommend using cilantro for the pesto, parsley or basil will also work.

Serves 4

2 medium sweet potatoes, peeled and cut into wedges

1½ tablespoons (23 ml) avocado or extra virgin olive oil, divided

Kosher salt and freshly ground black pepper

¾ cup (135 g) tricolor quinoa, rinsed

1⅓ cups (320 ml) water

2 medium summer squash, sliced

1 clove garlic, grated

1 bunch watercress, trimmed and chopped

2 cups (300 g) heirloom cherry tomatoes, halved

2 ears sweet corn, shucked and kernels removed

1 recipe Cilantro-Pumpkin Seed Pesto (page 19)

¼ cup (35 g) toasted pumpkin seeds

Get a head start! | The sweet potatoes and quinoa can be cooked in advance and reheated when you're ready to eat.

1 Preheat the oven to 425°F (220°C or gas mark 7).

2 Place the sweet potatoes on a rimmed baking sheet, drizzle with 1 tablespoon (15 ml) of the oil, sprinkle with salt and a few grinds of black pepper, and toss together. Spread in a single layer and roast until tender and lightly browned, tossing once halfway through, about 30 minutes total.

3 Meanwhile, place the quinoa, water, and a pinch of salt in a medium saucepan. Bring to a boil over medium-high heat, then reduce the heat to low, cover, and cook until tender, about 12 minutes. Remove from the heat and keep covered for 5 minutes. Fluff the quinoa with a fork.

4 Heat the remaining ½ tablespoon (8 ml) oil in a large skillet over medium heat. Add the summer squash and season with a pinch of salt and pepper. Cook, stirring occasionally, until just tender. Stir in the garlic and cook for 1 minute more.

5 To serve, divide the quinoa, sweet potatoes, summer squash, watercress, cherry tomatoes, and corn among four bowls. Spoon the Cilantro-Pumpkin Seed Pesto over the vegetables and sprinkle with the toasted pumpkin seeds.

Spicy Sesame Tofu and Broccoli Bowls

Tofu doesn't get much better than when it's partnered with a really good marinade. Here, cubed tofu gets soaked in an Asian-inspired marinade that gets a kick from a heaping spoonful of chili garlic sauce. The more time you can marinate the tofu, the more flavor it'll soak up. If there's any leftover marinade, go ahead and stir it into the tahini sauce—you won't regret it. For a less spicy version, reduce the chili garlic sauce to 1 teaspoon.

Serves 4

3 tablespoons (45 ml) soy sauce or tamari
1 tablespoon (15 ml) chili garlic sauce
2 teaspoons toasted sesame oil
1 teaspoon agave nectar
1 clove garlic, grated
14 ounces (392 g) extra-firm tofu, drained, pressed, and cubed
1 cup (165 g) brown basmati rice, rinsed
2 cups (480 ml) water
Kosher salt and freshly ground black pepper
1 tablespoon (8 g) cornstarch
½ small head red cabbage, cored and finely shredded
1 tablespoon (15 ml) avocado or extra virgin olive oil
1 medium head broccoli, cut into bite-size florets, steamed
1 recipe Miso Tahini Sauce (page 22)
4 scallions, thinly sliced
1 tablespoon (8 g) toasted sesame seeds

1 Stir together the soy sauce, chili garlic sauce, sesame oil, agave, and garlic in a shallow bowl or container. Add the tofu and gently toss to coat. Cover and marinate in the refrigerator for at least 30 minutes, up to overnight.

2 Preheat the oven to 400ºF (200ºC or gas mark 6). Line two baking sheets with parchment paper.

3 Combine the rice, water, and a pinch of salt in a medium saucepan. Bring to a boil over medium-high heat, then reduce the heat to low, cover, and simmer until tender and the water is absorbed, about 30 minutes.

4 Meanwhile, remove the tofu from the marinade, and if desired stir the remaining marinade into the Miso Tahini Sauce. Toss the tofu with the cornstarch. Arrange in a single layer on one of the prepared baking sheet. Cook until crispy, about 35 minutes, flipping once halfway through.

5 Add the cabbage to the second prepared baking sheet, drizzle with the oil, and sprinkle with salt and a few grinds of black pepper. Roast until tender, about 15 minutes.

6 To serve, divide the rice among four bowls. Top with the cabbage, tofu, and broccoli. Drizzle with the Miso Tahini Sauce and sprinkle with the scallions and sesame seeds.

Get a head start! | Prep the tofu and mix with the marinade up to a day in advance. You can also cook the rice, cabbage, and broccoli in advance and reheat when you're ready to eat.

Grilled Brassica Bowls

Last summer was the first time I cooked broccoli on the grill, and I was instantly smitten. The florets are wonderfully crisp and the stems just tender enough, but best of all is the smoky aroma you just can't get from roasting. While I typically trim broccoli into bite-size florets, here they're best cut into spears to prevent them from slipping through the grill grates. If you'd like a little extra insurance, go ahead and use a grill basket. Curly kale is a good option for grilling because the wavy edges pick up plenty of crispiness with a hint of char.

1 Place the kale in a large bowl. Drizzle 1 tablespoon (15 ml) of the oil over the kale leaves, sprinkle with salt and pepper, and massage into the leaves. Set aside while you heat the grill and prep the remaining vegetables.

2 Place the bulgur in a medium saucepan and toast over medium heat, stirring regularly, until lightly browned and fragrant, about 5 minutes. Stir in the water and a pinch of salt. Bring to a boil over medium-high heat, then reduce the heat to low, cover, and simmer until the bulgur is tender and the water is absorbed, about 10 minutes.

3 Meanwhile, preheat the grill to medium-high heat.

4 Stir together the remaining 2 tablespoons (30 ml) oil, soy sauce, and a few grinds of black pepper in a large bowl. Add the broccoli and kohlrabi and toss to coat. Place the broccoli and kohlrabi on the grill in a single layer over direct heat. Grill until lightly charred and crisp-tender, 8 to 10 minutes, turning once halfway through. Transfer to a plate and set aside.

5 Grill the kale until lightly charred around the edges, 1 to 2 minutes. Flip and grill for 1 minute more.

6 To serve, divide the grilled kale among four bowls. Top with the bulgur, grilled broccoli and kohlrabi, and avocado. Drizzle with the Miso-Ginger Sauce and sprinkle with the sunflower seeds.

Serves 4

1 bunch curly kale, center ribs
  removed
3 tablespoons (45 ml) avocado or
  extra virgin olive oil, divided
Kosher salt and freshly ground
  black pepper
½ cup (85 g) bulgur
1 cup (240 ml) water
2 tablespoons (30 ml) soy sauce
  or tamari
1 medium head broccoli, cut into
  large spears
2 kohlrabi, peeled and cut into ¼-inch
  (6 mm)-thick half-moons
1 avocado, peeled, pitted, and
  quartered lengthwise
1 recipe Miso-Ginger Sauce (page 20)
⅓ cup (45 g) unsalted toasted
  sunflower seeds

Get a head start! | The bulgur can be cooked in advance and reheated before serving.

RICE AND GRAIN
BOWLS

Turmeric Quinoa Bowls

I've been making these bowls for years, and it's high time I share them with you. Cooked in a mix of velvety coconut milk and broth and tinged with turmeric, the quinoa base is wonderfully rich. Partnered with bite-size pieces of spicy cauliflower, vinegar-kissed collard greens, pickled onion, and crunchy radishes, it's perfectly balanced—and that's what keeps me coming back again and again.

1 Arrange a rack in the middle of the oven and preheat to 425°F (220°C or gas mark 7).

2 Place the cauliflower on a rimmed baking sheet, drizzle with 1 tablespoon (15 ml) of the oil, sprinkle with the cayenne pepper and salt, and toss to combine. Roast until tender and lightly browned, about 20 minutes, stirring once halfway through.

3 Heat 1 tablespoon (15 ml) of the oil in a large saucepan over medium heat until shimmering. Add the onion and sauté until softened, about 5 minutes. Add the garlic, ginger, turmeric, and a pinch of salt, and cook until fragrant, about 1 minute. Stir in the quinoa, coconut milk, and ½ cup (120 ml) of the broth. Bring to a boil over medium-high heat, then reduce the heat to low, cover, and cook until tender and most of the liquid is absorbed, 12 to 15 minutes. Remove from the heat, stir in the peas, and keep covered for 5 minutes. Fluff with a fork.

4 Meanwhile, heat the remaining 1 tablespoon (15 ml) oil in a large skillet over medium heat. Add the collard greens and sauté until tender, about 5 minutes. Pour in the remaining ½ cup (120 ml) broth. Cook, stirring occasionally, for 5 minutes more. Remove from the heat and stir in the vinegar.

5 To serve, divide the quinoa among four bowls. Top with the cauliflower, collard greens, radishes, and pickled red onions. Drizzle with the Tahini Sauce.

Serves 4

1 medium head cauliflower (about 2 pounds [1820 g]), cut into bite-size florets
3 tablespoons (45 ml) avocado or extra virgin olive oil, divided
¼ teaspoon cayenne pepper
Kosher salt and freshly ground black pepper
1 small yellow onion, diced
2 cloves garlic
1 teaspoon chopped fresh ginger
1 teaspoon ground turmeric
1 cup (175 g) tricolor quinoa, rinsed
1 (14-ounce [392 g]) can unsweetened full-fat coconut milk
1 cup (240 ml) low-sodium vegetable broth, divided
1 cup (150 g) peas
1 large bunch collard greens (about 1½ pounds [680 g]), stems and center ribs removed and leaves chopped
1 teaspoon apple cider vinegar
1 bunch radishes, quartered
1 red onion, thinly sliced and pickled (page 25)
1 recipe Tahini Sauce (page 22)

Get a head start! | The cauliflower, quinoa, and collard greens can be cooked a day in advance and reheated before serving.

Mediterranean Farro Bowls

Sometimes the best bowl inspiration comes right from the grocery store. And in this case, it's my grocer's antipasto bar, which is loaded with briny olives, tangy peppadew peppers, savory marinated artichoke hearts, and so much more. The recipe calls for a couple cans of drained artichoke hearts, though thawed frozen artichokes or even marinated ones make a fine stand-in.

Serves 4

1 pint (300 g) grape tomatoes

2 (14-ounce [392 g]) cans quartered
   artichoke hearts, drained

1 large red onion, chopped

2 cloves garlic, smashed

2 tablespoons (30 ml) avocado or
   extra virgin olive oil, divided

Kosher salt and freshly ground
   black pepper

1 cup (175 g) farro, rinsed

1 cup (240 g) chickpeas, drained
   and rinsed

¼ cup (15 g) packed chopped
   fresh parsley leaves

2 tablespoons (8 g) chopped
   fresh oregano leaves

4 ounces (112 g) arugula

3 Persian cucumbers, chopped

¾ cup (75 g) pitted Kalamata olives

½ cup (50 g) peppadew peppers,
   thinly sliced

1 recipe Lemon-Caper Dressing
   (page 18)

1 Preheat the oven to 400°F (200°C or gas mark 6).

2 Place the tomatoes, drained artichoke hearts, onion, and garlic on a rimmed baking sheet. Drizzle with 1 tablespoon (15 ml) of the oil and sprinkle with salt and a few grinds of black pepper. Toss to combine and spread in an even layer. Roast until soft, about 30 minutes, tossing once halfway through.

3 Meanwhile, place the farro and a pinch of salt in a medium saucepan and cover with water by 2 inches (5 cm). Bring to a boil over medium-high heat, then reduce the heat and simmer, uncovered, until tender and slightly chewy, 10 to 15 minutes for pearled farro or 25 to 30 minutes for semi-pearled farro. Drain the excess water and return the farro to the pot. Add the remaining 1 tablespoon (15 ml) oil, chickpeas, parsley, and oregano, and stir together.

4 To serve, divide the arugula among four bowls. Top with the farro mixture, roasted vegetables, cucumbers, olives, and peppadews. Drizzle with the Lemon-Caper Dressing.

Get a head start! | The vegetables and farro can be cooked a day in advance and reheated before serving.

Cauliflower and Kimchi Fried Rice Bowls

Of all the ways to turn a bag of riced cauliflower into dinner, a batch of plant-based fried "rice" is at the top of my list. It picks up some punchy flavor from gut-friendly kimchi, and leans on quinoa and edamame for a boost of protein. And like all fried rice recipes, this version comes together quickly once you start cooking, so be sure to have all of the ingredients ready before stepping up to the stove.

Serves 4

2 tablespoons (30 ml) avocado or
    extra virgin olive oil, divided
1 bunch Tuscan kale, trimmed and
    chopped
1 small onion, diced
2 cloves garlic, minced
1½ cups (300 g) packed kimchi,
    drained and chopped, divided
1 pound (454 g) cauliflower rice,
    thawed if frozen
1 cup (185 g) cooked quinoa
4 scallions, thinly sliced, plus
    more for serving
½ teaspoon kosher salt
3 tablespoons (45 ml) soy sauce
    or tamari
2 cups (300 g) shelled edamame
Crumbled nori
Toasted sesame seeds

1 Heat 1 tablespoon (15 ml) of the oil in a wok or large nonstick skillet over medium-high heat until shimmering. Add the kale and cook, stirring occasionally, until tender, about 3 minutes. Transfer the kale to a bowl; set aside.

2 Heat the remaining 1 tablespoon (15 ml) oil in the same wok or skillet over medium-high heat until shimmering. Add the onion and garlic and stir-fry for 1 minute. Add ½ cup (100 g) of the kimchi and stir-fry until heated through, about 30 seconds. Add the cauliflower rice, quinoa, scallions, and salt and stir-fry for 3 minutes. Remove from the heat and stir in the remaining 1 cup (200 g) kimchi and the soy sauce.

3 To serve, divide the cauliflower rice among four bowls. Top with the kale, edamame, crumbled nori, sesame seeds, and additional scallions.

Spring Abundance Bowls

Even though I can usually find radishes, snap peas, and asparagus all year long, this bowl is never as good as when these vegetables hit their prime in spring. With fresh, bright, and vibrant flavors, this bowl is exactly what I want as the weather turns warmer and the sun shines brighter. I like to cut the asparagus spears into thirds so they're about the same size as the snap peas and easy to eat in one or two bites. Take your pick between eating this bowl with warm farro and asparagus, or make it in advance and eat it chilled—it's truly yummy both ways. If dairy is still part of your diet, crumbled feta also makes a nice topper for this bowl.

1 Place the farro and a pinch of salt in a medium saucepan and cover with water by 2 inches (5 cm). Bring to a boil over medium-high heat, then reduce the heat and simmer, uncovered, until tender and slightly chewy, 10 to 15 minutes for pearled farro or 25 to 30 minutes for semi-pearled farro. Drain the excess water and cool slightly.

2 Place the farro in a large bowl along with the watercress, mint, and scallions. Drizzle with ¼ cup (60 ml) of the Lemon Dressing and toss to combine.

3 To serve, divide the farro mixture among four bowls. Top with the asparagus, snap peas, radishes, and hazelnuts. Drizzle with the remaining dressing.

Serves 4

1 cup (175 g) farro, rinsed
Kosher salt
1 small bunch watercress, trimmed
    and chopped
¼ cup (15 g) fresh mint leaves
4 scallions, thinly sliced
1 recipe Lemon Dressing (page 18),
    divided
1 bunch asparagus, chopped
    and steamed
6 ounces (168 g) snap peas,
    halved crosswise
6 radishes, thinly sliced
⅓ cup (45 g) chopped toasted
    hazelnuts

Get a head start! | The farro and asparagus can be cooked in advance and, if desired, reheated when you're ready to eat.

BBQ Tofu Quinoa Bowls

There are two types of tofu bowls: the ones where you crisp up some cubes of tofu and toss them on top of your Buddha bowl and the ones where tofu gets a little more love to truly make it the shining star. These bowls fall firmly in the latter category. After the tofu is tossed with a warm, smoky spice rub, the craggy, bite-size chunks are roasted, then blanketed with a slick of your favorite BBQ sauce.

Serves 4

1 teaspoon ground cumin
1 teaspoon chili powder
1 teaspoon smoked paprika
1 teaspoon garlic powder
Kosher salt and freshly ground
    black pepper
2 tablespoons (30 ml) avocado or
    extra virgin olive oil, divided
14 ounces (392 g) extra-firm tofu,
    drained and pressed
¼ cup (60 ml) barbecue sauce
1 small head red cabbage (about
    1½ pounds [680 g]), cored and
    thinly sliced
1 cup (175 g) quinoa, rinsed
1¾ cups (420 ml) water
1 medium watermelon radish, thinly
    sliced and pickled (page 25)
2 avocados, peeled, pitted, and
    halved
1 recipe Tahini Sauce (page 22)

Get a head start! | The tofu, cabbage, and quinoa can be cooked a day in advance and reheated before serving. Toss the tofu with additional barbecue sauce, if desired.

1 Arrange oven racks to divide the oven into thirds and preheat to 425ºF (220ºC or gas mark 7). Line two baking sheets with parchment paper.

2 Stir together the spices, salt, a few grinds of black pepper, and 1 tablespoon (15 ml) of the oil in a medium bowl. Tear the tofu into bite-size pieces, add to the bowl, and toss to coat. Spread in a single layer on one of the prepared baking sheets. Roast until crisp, about 40 minutes, tossing halfway through. Pour the barbecue sauce over the tofu and toss to coat.

3 Meanwhile, add the cabbage to the second prepared baking sheet, drizzle with the remaining 1 tablespoon (15 ml) oil, and sprinkle with salt and a few grinds of black pepper. Toss to coat and spread in a single layer. Roast until tender, about 15 minutes.

4 Meanwhile, place the quinoa, water, and a pinch of salt in a medium saucepan. Bring to a boil over medium-high heat, reduce the heat to low, cover, and cook until tender, about 12 minutes. Remove from the heat and keep covered for 5 minutes. Fluff the quinoa with a fork.

5 To serve, divide the quinoa among four bowls. Top with the cabbage, tofu, watermelon radish, and avocado. Drizzle with the Tahini Sauce.

Autumn Harvest Bowls

When it comes to seasonal vegetables, most people can't stop gushing about the bounty of vibrant, fresh vegetables that come with summer. But for me, there is nothing more enjoyable than the root vegetables, hearty greens, and brassicas that take over with autumn's arrival. This bowl is a celebration of all my favorite fall things, like roasted carrots, parsnips, and Brussels sprouts, plus a crisp collard slaw tossed with shredded earthy beets, served with nutty wild rice.

1 Preheat the oven to 400°F (200°C or gas mark 6).

2 Place the rice and a pinch of salt in a medium saucepan and cover with water by 2 inches (5 cm). Bring to a boil over medium-high heat, then reduce the heat to low and simmer, uncovered, until chewy and some of the grains have burst, 40 to 50 minutes. Drain the excess water.

3 Meanwhile, in a large bowl, toss the Brussels sprouts, carrots, and parsnips with the oil, garlic powder, salt, and a few grinds of black pepper. Arrange in an even layer on two rimmed baking sheets. Roast until lightly browned, tossing halfway through, about 20 minutes total.

4 Place the shredded collard greens, shredded beet, and hemp seeds in a medium bowl with about ¼ cup (60 ml) of the Miso Tahini Sauce and toss to combine.

5 To serve, divide the collard green mixture among four bowls. Top with the wild rice, roasted vegetables, apple, pecans, and pumpkin seeds. Drizzle with the remaining sauce.

Serves 4

1 cup (175 g) wild rice, rinsed
Kosher salt and freshly ground
    black pepper
1 pound (455 g) Brussels sprouts,
    trimmed and halved
4 medium carrots, peeled and cut into
    2-inch (5 cm) sticks
4 medium parsnips, peeled and cut
    into 2-inch (5 cm) sticks
2 tablespoons (30 ml) avocado or
    extra virgin olive oil
1 teaspoon garlic powder
½ bunch collard greens, leaves finely
    shredded
1 medium beet, peeled and shredded
¼ cup (35 g) hemp seeds
1 recipe Miso Tahini Sauce (page 22),
    divided
1 large firm apple, cored and chopped
¼ cup (35 g) toasted pecans
¼ cup (35 g) toasted pumpkin seeds

Get a head start! | The rice can be cooked and the carrots, parsnips, and Brussels sprouts roasted in advance, stored separately, and reheated before serving.

Cauliflower-Polenta Bowls with Greens

If rich and creamy polenta is something you typically reserve for cold winter nights, this vibrant bowl will convince you to make it year-round. It packs in a serious cheesy flavor thanks to a few spoonfuls of nutritional yeast, while cauliflower rice keeps it on the lighter side. It's partnered with a tender mess of sautéed greens (and their stems!) and a punchy herb-packed sauce. If the greens are still attached to the beetroot, go ahead and cook them up with the chard.

1 Preheat the oven to 400°F (200°C or gas mark 6).

2 If the greens are still attached to the beetroot, separate, wash thoroughly, and set aside to cook with the chard. Scrub the beets, then peel and cube. Place the beets on one side of a rimmed baking sheet, drizzle with 1 tablespoon (15 ml) of the oil, and sprinkle with salt. Roast for 20 minutes. Remove from the oven and toss the beets. Place the fennel on the other side of the baking sheet, drizzle with ½ tablespoon (7.5 ml) of the oil, sprinkle with salt, and toss to coat. Roast until tender, about 20 minutes more.

3 Meanwhile, heat 1 tablespoon (15 ml) of the oil in a large saucepan over medium heat until shimmering. Add the cauliflower rice, season with a pinch of salt, and cook for 5 minutes. Pour in the broth and bring to a boil over medium-high heat. Slowly whisk in the cornmeal and a generous pinch of salt. Reduce the heat to low and stir constantly until thickened, about 2 minutes. Cover and cook, stirring every 10 minutes and scraping the bottom and corners of the pot, until creamy, about 30 minutes. Remove from the heat and stir in the nutritional yeast.

4 Meanwhile, heat the remaining ½ tablespoon (7.5 ml) oil in a Dutch oven over medium heat until shimmering. Add the rainbow chard greens and stems (and beet greens, if using) and a pinch of salt, and sauté until tender, about 5 minutes. Add the garlic and cook for 1 minute longer.

5 To serve, divide the polenta among four bowls. Top with the chard, roasted beets, and fennel. Spoon the Chimichurri Sauce over the top and sprinkle with the toasted pumpkin seeds.

Serves 4

1 bunch red beets
3 tablespoons (45 ml) avocado or extra virgin olive oil, divided
Kosher salt and freshly ground black pepper
1 large or 2 small heads fennel (about 1 pound [455])), trimmed and chopped
2 cups (240 g) cauliflower rice
4 cups (960 ml) low-sodium vegetable broth
1 cup (140 g) coarse cornmeal
3 tablespoons (15 g) nutritional yeast
1 large bunch rainbow chard, greens and stems chopped
2 cloves garlic, minced
1 recipe Chimichurri Sauce (page 12)
¼ cup (35 g) toasted pumpkin seeds

Get a head start! | The beets and fennel can be roasted and the chard sautéed in advance, then reheated when ready to serve.

Asparagus and Mushroom Stir-Fry Bowls

Even though you can buy asparagus any time of the year, there is nothing quite like what you'll find in the springtime when asparagus is in its prime, with wonderfully crisp spears and a fresh, grassy aroma. If you can, grab a bunch of thin spears, which are quicker cooking and more tender. And like any stir-fry, this one comes together in a flash, so have all your ingredients ready before you start cooking.

Serves 4

1 cup (175 g) brown basmati rice
2¼ cups (600 ml) water, divided
Kosher salt and freshly ground
   black pepper
3 tablespoons (45 ml) soy sauce
   or tamari
2 teaspoons rice vinegar
2 teaspoons mirin
1 teaspoon sesame oil
1 teaspoon cornstarch
2 tablespoons (30 ml) avocado or
   extra virgin olive oil, divided
1 pound (455 g) mixed mushrooms,
   such as cremini, shiitake, oyster,
   and maitake, sliced
1 bunch asparagus, trimmed and
   cut into 1-inch (2.5 cm) pieces
8 ounces (225 g) sliced water
   chestnuts
¾ cup (105 g) chopped unsalted
   toasted cashews
2 cloves garlic, grated
1-inch (2.5 cm) piece ginger,
   peeled and julienned
1 tablespoon (9 g) toasted black
   sesame seeds, plus more
   for topping
Pinch of red pepper flakes

1 Add the rice, 2 cups (480 ml) of the water, and a pinch of salt to a medium saucepan and bring to a boil over medium-high heat. Reduce the heat to low, cover, and cook until the rice is tender and the liquid is absorbed, about 30 minutes. Remove from the heat and steam the rice with the lid on for 5 minutes.

2 Whisk together the remaining ¼ cup (60 ml) water, soy sauce, rice vinegar, mirin, sesame oil, and cornstarch in a small bowl until the cornstarch is dissolved. Set aside.

3 Heat 1½ tablespoons (23 ml) of the oil in a wok or large frying pan over medium-high heat until very hot but not smoking. Add the mushrooms and stir-fry until lightly browned, about 5 minutes. Transfer to a plate; set aside.

4 Pour the remaining ½ tablespoon (7 ml) of oil into the pan. Add the asparagus, season with salt and a few grinds of black pepper, and stir-fry for 2 minutes. Add the water chestnuts, cashews, garlic, ginger, sesame seeds, and red pepper flakes, and stir-fry for 1 minute longer.

5 Stir together the sauce once more to dissolve the cornstarch. Return the mushrooms to the pan. Pour the sauce over the vegetables and cook for 1 minute, stirring constantly.

6 To serve, divide the rice among four bowls, top with the stir-fry, and sprinkle with more toasted sesame seeds.

Get a head start! | The rice can be cooked a day in advance and reheated before serving.

Fattoush Salad Bowls with Bulgur and Hummus

Inspired by fattoush, the Middle Eastern bread salad starring toasted pita, plenty of fresh herbs, and sumac-spiked lemon vinaigrette, this bowl is wholesome, hearty, and packed with fresh, bright flavor. Hummus and bulgur aren't traditional accompaniments to fattoush, but they do a nice job of rounding out this meal. And if you're not totally ruling out dairy, I happen to think crumbled feta is also a nice touch.

Serves 4

¾ cup (120 g) bulgur
1½ cups (360 ml) water
Kosher salt
4 pita breads
2 teaspoons extra virgin olive oil
1 teaspoon ground sumac, plus
   more for garnish
1 heart romaine, chopped
½ packed cup (30 g) fresh parsley
   leaves, chopped
½ packed cup (30 g) fresh mint
   leaves, chopped
4 Persian cucumbers, sliced
1½ cups (225 g) cherry tomatoes,
   halved
6 radishes, thinly sliced
1 recipe Sumac Lemon Dressing
   (page 18), divided
1 recipe Creamy Hummus (page 17)

1 Preheat the oven to 350°F (180°C or gas mark 4).

2 Place the bulgur, water, and a pinch of salt in a medium saucepan. Bring to a boil over medium-high heat, then reduce the heat to low, cover, and simmer until tender, 10 to 15 minutes.

3 Meanwhile, brush the pita with the oil and sprinkle with the ground sumac and a pinch of salt. Arrange in a single layer on a baking sheet. Bake until crisp and golden brown, about 15 minutes. When cool enough to handle, break into bite-size pieces.

4 Combine the lettuce, herbs, cucumbers, tomatoes, and radishes in a large bowl. Drizzle with ¼ cup (60 ml) of the Sumac Lemon Dressing and toss to combine. Stir in half of the broken pita chips.

5 To serve, spread a layer of the Creamy Hummus over the bottom and sides of four bowls. Divide the salad among the bowls and top with a scoop of bulgur. Drizzle with the remaining dressing, top with the remaining pita chips, and sprinkle with additional ground sumac, if desired.

Get a head start! | The pita can be made up to several days in days and will keep well in an airtight container. The bulgur can be cooked a day in advance and reheated when you're ready to serve.

Orzo Bowls with Arugula Pesto

Sometimes the most inspiring bowls happen when you're pulling odds and ends from the pantry and fridge, and what comes together is a bowl that's far more magical and delicious than you ever imagined. Like this one, which was born from my love of pesto pasta salad. Rice-shaped orzo serves as the base and gets bolstered with tender sautéed mushrooms, grape tomatoes, and fresh baby spinach, then topped off with a shower of crunchy roasted chickpeas.

1 Cook the orzo in a pot of boiling water according to the package directions, until just al dente. Drain well and set aside.

2 Heat the oil in the same pot over medium heat. Add the onion and sauté, stirring occasionally, until softened, about 5 minutes. Add the mushrooms and tomatoes. Cook, stirring occasionally, until the mushrooms have released their juices and the tomatoes are softened, about 8 minutes. Stir in the spinach and cook until just wilted, about 2 minutes. Return the orzo to the pot along with the Arugula-Cashew Pesto Sauce. Stir into the vegetables, breaking up any clumps of orzo, and cook until heated through.

3 To serve, divide the orzo mixture among four bowls and top with the roasted chickpeas.

Serves 4

8 ounces (225 g) dried orzo

2 tablespoons (30 ml) extra virgin olive oil

1 small red onion, diced

8 ounces (225 g) cremini mushrooms, sliced

1 pint (300 g) grape tomatoes, halved

5 ounces (140 g) baby spinach, chopped

1 recipe Arugula-Cashew Pesto Sauce (page 19)

½ cup (120 g) roasted chickpeas

Sweet Potato and Wild Rice Bowls

If you ask me, wild rice is a totally underrated and underused grain, and we could all stand to add it to Buddha bowls more often. It also happens to be one of my favorite bowl bases, and a fun fact that most people don't know is that, despite the name, wild rice isn't actually a type of rice at all. Instead, it's a species of grass with edible seeds that look just like grains of rice. Here it serves as the base to crispy roasted sweet potatoes and a duo of sautéed kale and radicchio, and gets finished off with an herby tahini sauce.

Serves 4

1 cup (160 g) wild rice, rinsed
Kosher salt and freshly ground
    black pepper
2 medium sweet potatoes, peeled
    and cut into wedges
2 tablespoons (30 ml) avocado or
    extra virgin olive oil, divided
1 small bunch Tuscan kale, leaves
    shredded
1 small head radicchio, cored and
    chopped
1 teaspoon ground coriander
4 radishes, thinly sliced
1 recipe Green Tahini Sauce (page 22)
2 tablespoons (16 g) toasted
    sesame seeds
2 tablespoons (16 g) hemp seeds

1 Preheat the oven to 425ºF (220ºC or gas mark 7).

2 Place the rice and a pinch of salt in a medium saucepan and cover with water by 2 inches (5 cm). Bring to a boil over medium-high heat, then reduce the heat to low and simmer, uncovered, until chewy and some of the grains have burst, 40 to 50 minutes. Drain the excess water.

3 Meanwhile, place the sweet potatoes on a rimmed baking sheet, drizzle with 1 tablespoon (15 ml) of the oil, sprinkle with salt and a few grinds of black pepper, and toss to coat. Spread in a single layer and roast until tender and lightly browned, tossing once halfway through, 25 to 30 minutes total.

4 Heat the remaining 1 tablespoon (15 ml) oil in a large skillet over medium heat until shimmering. Add the kale and sauté until tender, about 5 minutes. Add the radicchio and ground coriander and cook for 2 minutes more.

5 To serve, divide the wild rice among four bowls. Top with the kale and radicchio mixture, sweet potatoes, and radishes. Drizzle with the Green Tahini Sauce and sprinkle with the sesame seeds and hemp seeds.

Get a head start! | The rice and sweet potatoes can be cooked a day in advance and reheated before serving.

Brown Rice and Broccoli Goddess Bowls

These smoky yet bright bowls were born from my love of blissfully creamy Avocado Green Goddess Dressing. Traditionally made with mayo, this lightened-up version of the classic dressing starts with ripe avocado, loads up on fresh herbs, and finishes with just enough tangy lemon juice to make the perfect partner to charred broccoli. While there are several methods for making charred broccoli, I happen to be partial to the broiler because it's quick, low effort, and doesn't require too much watching over. The total cook time for the broccoli will vary depending on the power of your broiler, so check it about every 5 minutes or so.

1 Place the rice, water, and a pinch of salt in a medium saucepan and bring to a boil over medium-high heat. Reduce the heat to low, cover, and cook until the rice is tender, 30 to 40 minutes.

2 Meanwhile, set an oven rack 6 inches (15 cm) under the broiler and set the oven to broil. Place the broccoli on a large rimmed baking sheet, drizzle with the oil, and season with salt and a few grinds of black pepper. Toss to coat the broccoli and arrange in a single layer. Char the broccoli under the broiler until lightly browned around the edges and crisp-tender, 10 to 15 minutes total, stirring every 5 minutes. Remove the baking sheet from the oven. Pour the lemon juice and sprinkle the red pepper flakes over the broccoli and toss.

3 To serve, divide the brown rice among four bowls. Top with the charred broccoli, sliced radish, and quick-pickled shredded carrot. Drizzle with the Avocado Green Goddess Dressing and garnish with the Savory Seed Sprinkle.

Serves 4

1 cup (165 g) brown rice, preferably short grain

2 cups (480 ml) water

Kosher salt and freshly ground black pepper

1 large crown broccoli, cut into bite-size florets

2 tablespoons (30 ml) avocado or extra virgin olive oil

2 tablespoons (30 ml) freshly squeezed lemon juice

¼ teaspoon red pepper flakes

1 medium watermelon radish, thinly sliced

1 cup (110 g) shredded carrot, pickled (page 25)

1 recipe Avocado Green Goddess Dressing (page 13)

⅓ cup (45 g) Savory Seed Sprinkle (page 16)

Get a head start! | The brown rice can be made a day ahead and reheated before serving. The pickled carrot, dressing, and Savory Seed Sprinkle can all be made in advance.

Summer Farro Bowls

For the first time in my adult life, I have a tomato plant on my patio. Cherry tomatoes. And it's flourishing more than I ever expected. As I've eaten them up in just about every way imaginable (and still barely making a dent in the bounty), I find myself coming back to this bowl more than anything else. It's inspired by succotash and everything I crave during summer.

Serves 4

1 cup (165 g) farro, rinsed
Kosher salt and freshly ground
 black pepper
Zest and juice from 1 lemon
¼ cup (15 g) finely chopped fresh
 mint leaves
¼ cup (15 g) finely chopped fresh
 basil leaves
1 tablespoon (15 ml) avocado or
 extra virgin olive oil
2 shallots, diced
1 clove garlic, minced
2 small summer squash or zucchini,
 chopped
2 ears sweet summer corn, kernels
 removed
1 cup (150 g) frozen lima beans,
 thawed
1 cup (150 g) cherry tomatoes, halved
2 ounces (56 g) arugula
1 recipe Avocado Sauce (page 14)

1 Place the farro and a pinch of salt in a medium saucepan and cover with water by 2 inches (5 cm). Bring to a boil over medium-high heat, then reduce the heat and simmer, uncovered, until tender and slightly chewy, 10 to 15 minutes for pearled farro or 25 to 30 minutes for semi-pearled farro. Drain the excess water and transfer the farro to a large bowl. Once cool, stir in the lemon zest and juice, mint, and basil.

2 Meanwhile, heat the oil in a large skillet over medium heat until shimmering. Add the shallot and garlic and sauté until softened, about 3 minutes. Add the summer squash and cook, stirring occasionally, until barely tender, about 5 minutes. Add the corn, lima beans, tomatoes, a pinch of salt, and a few grinds of black pepper and cook until heated through and tender, about 5 minutes more.

3 To serve, divide the arugula among four bowls. Top with the farro, followed by the sautéed vegetables, and drizzle with the Avocado Sauce.

Tempeh Teriyaki Rice Bowls

Inspired by the takeout classic, this plant-based riff on teriyaki bowls starts with sweet and savory homemade teriyaki sauce that clings to the pieces of seared tempeh. You could call it a day with that sauce alone, but I don't recommend that. Go ahead and drizzle on the Miso-Ginger Sauce, too! The savory umami-rich flavor is a great complement to the teriyaki sauce, and you'll love the way it seeps between the layers of the roasted Brussels sprouts.

1 Preheat the oven to 400°F (200°C or gas mark 6).

2 Place the rice, 2 cups (480 ml) of the water, and a pinch of salt in a medium saucepan and bring to a boil over medium-high heat. Reduce the heat to low, cover, and simmer, stirring occasionally, until the rice is tender and the water is absorbed, about 30 minutes.

3 Meanwhile, place the mushrooms and Brussels sprouts on a rimmed baking sheet, drizzle with 1 tablespoon (15 ml) of the oil, sprinkle with a pinch of salt and a few grinds of black pepper, and toss to coat. Roast until tender and lightly browned, about 20 minutes, stirring once halfway through.

4 Meanwhile, whisk together the soy sauce, rice vinegar, honey, remaining 1 tablespoon (15 ml) water, cornstarch, ginger, and garlic in a small bowl. Set aside.

5 Heat the remaining 1 tablespoon (15 ml) oil in a large skillet over medium-high heat until shimmering. Add the tempeh, season with a pinch of salt and a few grinds of black pepper, and cook, stirring often, until heated through, about 3 minutes. Whisk the reserved sauce, pour over the tempeh, and cook until the sauce is slightly thickened.

6 To serve, divide the rice among four bowls. Top with the tempeh, roasted mushrooms and Brussels sprouts, and radishes. Drizzle with the Miso-Ginger Sauce.

Serves 4

1 cup (165 g) forbidden rice

2 cups (480 ml) plus 1 tablespoon (15 ml) water, divided

Kosher salt and freshly ground black pepper

8 ounces (225 g) cremini mushrooms, quartered

8 ounces (225 g) Brussels sprouts, trimmed and halved

2 tablespoons (30 ml) avocado or extra virgin olive oil, divided

3 tablespoons (45 ml) soy sauce or tamari

2 tablespoons (30 ml) rice vinegar

1 tablespoon (20 g) honey

1 tablespoon (8 g) cornstarch

2 teaspoons finely grated fresh ginger

2 cloves garlic, grated

8 ounces (225 g) tempeh

6 radishes, thinly sliced

1 recipe Miso-Ginger Sauce (page 20)

Get a head start! | The rice can be cooked a day in advance and reheated before serving.

LENTIL AND BEAN
BOWLS

Tomato-Braised Butter Bean Bowls

What started as a humble meal to clean out my pantry and turn a can of butter beans into dinner nearly ten years ago slowly turned into a rich and hearty meal that I still eat all the time. If you're not familiar with butter beans, I hope I can help change that. A variety of lima bean, butter beans are large and flat with yellowish-white coloring, and a seriously meaty bite. Here, they get sautéed with sweet onion, simmered in a bath of diced tomatoes and herbs, then partnered with garlicky kale and mushrooms.

Serves 4

¾ cup (120 g) millet

1½ cups (360 ml) water

Kosher salt and freshly ground
    black pepper

2 tablespoons (30 ml) extra virgin
    olive oil, divided

1 small onion, diced

3 cups (720 ml) or 2 (15-ounce
    [420 g]) cans butter beans,
    drained and rinsed

1 (28-ounce [784 g]) can fire-roasted
    diced tomatoes

2 teaspoons dried thyme

2 teaspoons dried oregano

Pinch of red pepper flakes

8 ounces (225 g) cremini mushrooms,
    quartered

4 packed cups (280 g) shredded
    Tuscan kale leaves

2 cloves garlic, minced

Get a head start! | The millet, braised beans, and sautéed vegetables can be cooked in advance and reheated before serving.

1 Add the millet to a large, dry saucepan and toast over medium heat until golden brown, 4 to 5 minutes. Add the water and a pinch of salt. The water will sputter but will settle down quickly. Bring to a boil over medium-high heat, then reduce the heat to low, cover, and simmer until most of the water is absorbed, 15 to 20 minutes. Remove from the heat and steam in the pot for 5 minutes.

2 Meanwhile, heat 1 tablespoon (15 ml) of the oil in a large skillet over medium-high heat until shimmering. Add the onion and cook, stirring occasionally, until softened, about 3 minutes. Add the beans, season with a pinch of salt and a few grinds of black pepper, spread in an even layer, and cook undisturbed until the bottoms are lightly browned, about 3 minutes. Stir in the diced tomatoes and juices, dried herbs, and red pepper flakes. Reduce the heat to low and simmer for 15 minutes.

3 Meanwhile, heat the remaining 1 tablespoon (15 ml) oil in a separate large skillet over medium heat until shimmering. Add the mushrooms, season with a pinch of salt and a few grinds of black pepper, and cook, stirring occasionally, until softened, 6 to 8 minutes. Add the kale and garlic and cook, tossing occasionally, until wilted, 2 to 3 minutes.

4 To serve, divide the millet among four bowls. Top with the braised beans and the kale and mushrooms.

Lentil and Delicata Squash Chimichurri Bowls

You know when you start eating something, and just one or two bites in, you already never want it to end? That's how I feel every single time I tuck into this bowl. Work a little bit of everything onto your fork—the sweet, caramelized winter squash, briny olives, peppery arugula, and vibrant chimichurri, maybe a slice of crunchy beet—and you'll see what I'm talking about. These ingredients are all great on their own, but combine them together in a sweet, salty, savory tangle, and they're far greater than the sum of their parts.

1 Preheat the oven to 425°F (220°C or gas mark 7).

2 Cut each squash in half lengthwise. Scoop out the seeds. Slice each squash crosswise into ½-inch (1.3 cm)-thick crescents. Place on a rimmed baking sheet, drizzle with the oil, season with a pinch of salt and a few grinds of black pepper, and toss to coat. Arrange in a single layer and roast until tender and lightly browned all over, about 20 minutes, flipping once halfway through.

3 Meanwhile, place the lentils, garlic, and a pinch of salt in a medium saucepan and cover with water by 2 inches (5 cm). Bring to a boil over medium-high heat, then reduce the heat to low and simmer until the lentils are tender, about 25 minutes. Drain, remove and discard the garlic, and set aside.

4 Meanwhile, place the quinoa, water, and a pinch of salt in a medium saucepan. Bring to a boil over medium-high heat, then reduce the heat to low, cover, and cook until tender, about 10 minutes. Remove from the heat and keep covered for 5 minutes. Fluff the quinoa with a fork.

5 To serve, spread a heaping spoonful of Chimichurri Sauce in the bottom of four bowls, then cover with the arugula. Top with the lentils, quinoa, roasted delicata squash, beets, olives, and pumpkin seeds. Spoon the remaining Chimichurri Sauce over the top.

Serves 4

3 medium delicata squash
1 tablespoon (15 ml) avocado or extra virgin olive oil
Kosher salt and freshly ground black pepper
1 cup (190 g) French lentils, rinsed
1 clove garlic, peeled and smashed
½ cup (85 g) quinoa, rinsed
¾ cup (180 ml) water
1 recipe Chimichurri Sauce (page 12), divided
2 packed cups (60 g) arugula
1 large beet, peeled and thinly sliced
½ cup (50 g) pitted Castelvetrano olives, smashed
¼ cup (35 g) toasted pumpkin seeds

Get a head start! | The squash can be roasted and lentils and quinoa cooked in advance, stored separately, and reheated before serving.

Chickpea and Cauliflower Masala Bowls

On cold winter nights when you're craving pure comfort and a hearty meal that will warm you up from the inside out, this is the recipe to turn to. It delivers every single time. The combination of fragrant spices, like garam masala, coriander, and turmeric, along with fresh ginger and a little kick of heat from the serrano chile, will warm your belly, while baby spinach, cauliflower, and fresh cilantro add balance to keep dinner from feeling too heavy.

Serves 4

1 tablespoon (15 ml) virgin coconut oil
1 medium onion, diced
1 tablespoon (8 g) finely grated
　fresh ginger
2 cloves garlic, grated
1 small serrano chile, seeded and
　diced (optional)
2 teaspoons garam masala
1 teaspoon ground coriander
½ teaspoon ground turmeric
Kosher salt and freshly ground
　black pepper
1 small head cauliflower, cut into
　small florets
3 cups (720 ml) or 2 (15-ounce
　[420 g]) cans chickpeas, drained
　and rinsed
1 (28-ounce [784 g]) can fire-roasted
　diced tomatoes
1½ cups (360 ml) water
1 cup (165 g) white basmati rice,
　rinsed
5 ounces (140 g) baby spinach,
　steamed
¼ cup (4 g) chopped fresh cilantro
　leaves and tender stems
2 tablespoons (16 g) sliced toasted
　almonds
2 tablespoons (10 g) unsweetened
　toasted coconut flakes

1 Heat the oil in a Dutch oven over medium heat until shimmering. Add the onion and cook, stirring occasionally, until softened, about 5 minutes. Add the ginger, garlic, chile (if using), garam masala, coriander, turmeric, a pinch of salt, and a few grinds of black pepper and stir to combine. Cook until fragrant, about 2 minutes. Stir in the cauliflower florets, chickpeas, and tomatoes. Bring to a boil over medium-high heat, then reduce the heat to low and simmer for 25 minutes, stirring occasionally.

2 Meanwhile, bring the water to a boil in a medium saucepan. Stir in the rice, reduce the heat to low, cover, and simmer until the rice is tender and the water is absorbed, about 15 minutes.

3 To serve, divide the rice among four bowls. Top with the chickpea and cauliflower mixture and steamed spinach. Sprinkle with the cilantro, almonds, and coconut flakes.

Get a head start! | The chickpea and cauliflower mixture and rice can be cooked in advance, stored separately, and reheated before serving.

Lentil Niçoise Bowls

I was first introduced to classic Niçoise salad during my culinary school days and instantly found the mix of fresh vegetables, briny ingredients, and tangy vinaigrette alluring and intoxicating. These bowls are a vibrant and fresh twist on the traditional French salad, swapping the tuna for meaty, toothsome lentils and the buttery lettuce for peppery arugula, while tossing in radishes for crunch and finishing it off with a sunny Lemon-Caper Dressing.

1 Preheat the oven to 425°F (220°C or gas mark 7).

2 Place the potatoes on a rimmed baking sheet, add 1 tablespoon (15 ml) of the oil and the garlic powder, season with salt and a few grinds of black pepper, and toss to coat. Spread in an even layer. Roast until tender and lightly browned, tossing halfway through, about 20 minutes total.

3 Place the lentils and a pinch of salt in a medium saucepan and cover with water by at least 2 inches (5 cm). Bring to a boil over medium-high heat, then reduce the heat to low, cover, and simmer until tender, about 25 minutes. Drain the excess water.

4 Meanwhile, heat the remaining 1 tablespoon (15 ml) oil in a large skillet over medium heat until shimmering. Add the shallot and sauté until softened, about 3 minutes. Add the green beans and season with a pinch of salt and pepper. Cook, stirring occasionally, until just tender, about 5 minutes.

5 To serve, divide the arugula and lentils among four bowls. Top with the potatoes, green beans, radishes, and olives. Drizzle with the Lemon-Caper Dressing and sprinkle with the chives.

Serves 4

1 pound (455 g) tricolor new
  potatoes, halved
2 tablespoons (30 ml) extra virgin
  olive oil, divided
½ teaspoon garlic powder
Kosher salt and freshly ground
  black pepper
¾ cup (140 g) French lentils
1 shallot, diced
8 ounces (225 g) green beans,
  trimmed
4 ounces (112 g) arugula
1 small bunch radishes, quartered
½ cup (50 g) pitted Niçoise or
  kalamata olives
1 recipe Lemon-Caper Dressing
  (page 18)
1 tablespoon (1 g) minced chives

Get a head start! | The potatoes, lentils, and green beans can be cooked a day in advance and reheated before serving.

Harissa Green Bean Bowls with Whipped Tahini

My absolute favorite way to eat this Mediterranean-inspired bowl is with a little bit of everything piled on my fork—a couple of tender roasted green beans, a slice or two of pickled fennel, a few unwieldy strands of raw cabbage, as much freekeh as I can nestle in between the vegetables, and of course a dollop of whipped tahini on top. It's spicy, acidic, nutty, creamy, and crunchy all at once, and it's so delightful.

1 Place the freekeh in a medium saucepan and toast over medium heat until fragrant, about 3 minutes. Pour in the water and a pinch of salt and bring to a boil over medium-high heat. Reduce the heat to low, cover, and simmer until tender and the water is absorbed, 20 to 25 minutes. Remove from the heat and steam for 10 minutes. Fluff with a fork.

2 Meanwhile, heat the oil in a large skillet over medium-high heat until shimmering. Add the green beans and a pinch of salt and cook, tossing occasionally, until lightly browned. Add the harissa, toss to coat, and cook for about 3 minutes longer.

3 To serve, divide the freekeh among four bowls. Top with the green beans, red cabbage, avocado, pickled fennel, and Whipped Tahini, and sprinkle with the sliced almonds and hemp seeds.

Serves 4

1 cup (160 g) cracked freekeh
2½ cups (600 ml) water
Kosher salt and freshly ground black pepper
1 tablespoon (15 ml) avocado or extra virgin olive oil
1 pound (455 g) green beans, trimmed
1 tablespoon (15 g) harissa paste
2 cups (140 g) finely shredded red cabbage
1 avocado, peeled, pitted, and sliced
1 medium fennel bulb, thinly sliced and pickled (page 25)
1 recipe Whipped Tahini (page 23)
¼ cup (35 g) sliced toasted almonds
2 tablespoons (16 g) hemp seeds

Get a head start! | The freekeh can be cooked a day in advance and reheated before serving.

Cuban-Style Black Bean Bowls

Just as you'd expect, these Cuban-style black beans are simmered with onion, bell pepper, garlic, and smoky spices. But instead of being served up as a side dish, they're the star of the show and partnered with cilantro-lime rice to make a complete protein. Toppings like tangy pickled red cabbage, chopped radishes, and plantain chips give the bowl a big pop of bright flavor and some added crunch.

Serves 4

1 cup (165 g) white basmati rice, rinsed

2½ cups (600 ml) water, divided

1 tablespoon (15 ml) freshly squeezed lime juice

¼ cup (4 g) chopped fresh cilantro leaves, plus more for topping

1 tablespoon (15 ml) avocado or extra virgin olive oil

1 small red onion, diced

1 green bell pepper, cored, seeded, and diced

2 cloves garlic, minced

3 cups (720 ml) or 2 (15-ounce [420 g]) cans black beans, drained and rinsed

1 teaspoon ground cumin

1 teaspoon dried oregano

1 bay leaf

Kosher salt and freshly ground black pepper

8 ounces (225 g) shredded red cabbage, pickled (page 25)

1 small bunch radishes, chopped

2 avocados, peeled, pitted, and thinly sliced

Plantain chips

Lime wedges

1 Combine the rice and 2 cups (480 ml) of the water in a medium saucepan. Bring to a boil over medium-high heat, then reduce the heat to low, cover, and simmer until the rice is tender and the water is absorbed, 15 to 18 minutes. Remove from the heat and stir in the lime juice and cilantro.

2 Meanwhile, heat the oil in a large saucepan over medium heat until shimmering. Add the onion, bell pepper, and garlic and sauté until the vegetables are softened, about 5 minutes. Stir in the remaining ½ cup (120 ml) water, black beans, cumin, oregano, bay leaf, a pinch of salt, and a few grinds of black pepper. Cook until fragrant, stirring occasionally, about 10 minutes. Remove and discard the bay leaf.

3 To serve, divide the rice and pickled cabbage among four bowls. Top with the black beans, radishes, avocado, plantain chips, and a lime wedge.

Get a head start! | The rice and beans can be cooked a day in advance, stored separately, and reheated before serving.

Marinated Celery and Kidney Bean Bowls

While I love the convenience of canned beans, these bowls are a time I always prefer to plan ahead and use dried beans. They have a more toothsome bite that I really love and that works well with the mix of ingredients in the bowl. There's absolutely nothing wrong with canned kidney beans, though. They come with a convenience factor that can't be beat and work just as well here. Celery leaves are an oft-overlooked part of this stalked vegetable, and I happen to love them. Here you'll use them to top off the bowl. Don't have any? Parsley makes a nice substitute.

Serves 4

3 tablespoons (45 ml) sherry vinegar
Juice from ½ lemon
2 teaspoons Dijon mustard
½ teaspoon Aleppo pepper
Kosher salt
¼ cup (60 ml) extra virgin olive oil
3 cups (720 ml) or 2 (15-ounce [420 g]) cans kidney beans, drained and rinsed
6 large stalks celery, sliced on the diagonal and leaves reserved (about 3 cups [330 g])
1 shallot, thinly sliced
2 cloves garlic, peeled and smashed
¾ cup (120 g) farro, rinsed
1 small apple, cored and julienned
1 small bunch radishes, thinly sliced
¼ packed cup (15 g) chopped celery leaves or fresh parsley leaves
⅓ cup (45 g) chopped toasted walnuts

1 Whisk together the vinegar, lemon juice, mustard, Aleppo pepper, and a pinch of salt in a large bowl. Slowly drizzle in the olive oil, whisking constantly until emulsified. Add the kidney beans, sliced celery, shallot, and garlic. Stir to coat. Cover and marinate in the refrigerator for at least 1 hour. Remove the garlic from the bowl and discard.

2 Meanwhile, place the farro and a pinch of salt in a medium saucepan and cover with water by 2 inches (5 cm). Bring to a boil over medium-high heat, then reduce the heat and simmer, uncovered, until tender and slightly chewy, 10 to 15 minutes for pearled farro or 25 to 30 minutes for semi-pearled farro. Drain the excess water.

3 To serve, divide the marinated beans and celery among four bowls. Top with the farro, julienned apple, radishes, celery leaves, and walnuts.

Get a head start! | The farro can be cooked a day in advance and, if desired, reheated before serving.

Cauliflower Rice and Black Bean Burrito Bowls

Here, cauliflower rice takes the place of regular rice to work even more veggies into your bowl. Inspired by restaurant-style Mexican rice, the cauliflower is tinged with a smoky tomato flavor, a touch of heat, and a squeeze of lime. I prefer fresh cauliflower rice here because it has a little more bite, but a bag of the frozen stuff will work just fine.

1 Heat the oil in a large skillet over medium heat until shimmering. Add the onion and sauté until softened, about 5 minutes. Stir in the cauliflower rice, garlic, jalapeño (if using), cumin, a pinch of salt, and a few grinds of black pepper. Cook, stirring occasionally, until the cauliflower is tender, 3 to 5 minutes. Add the tomato paste, stir to coat the cauliflower rice, and cook for 2 minutes more. Remove from the heat and stir in the cilantro and lime juice.

2 To serve, divide the chopped romaine and cauliflower rice among four bowls. Top with the black beans, corn, salsa, and more cilantro and drizzle with the Avocado Sauce. If desired, top with crumbled tortilla chips.

Serves 4

2 tablespoons (30 ml) avocado or extra virgin olive oil

1 small onion, diced

1 pound (455 g) cauliflower rice, fresh or frozen

2 cloves garlic, minced

1 small jalapeño pepper, seeded and diced (optional)

2 teaspoons ground cumin

Kosher salt and freshly ground black pepper

1 tablespoon (15 g) tomato paste

¼ cup (4 g) chopped fresh cilantro, plus more for topping

Juice from ½ lime

1 heart romaine, chopped

3 cups (720 ml) or 2 (15-ounce [420 g]) cans black beans, drained and rinsed

1 cup (150 g) corn kernels, preferably fresh

1 cup (240 ml) salsa

1 recipe Avocado Sauce (page 14)

Tortilla chips (optional)

Sicilian Cauliflower Bowls with Kidney Beans and Orzo

There's a chance you may never see roasted cauliflower the same way after tasting this bowl. While the cauliflower roasts, mix together the dressing and prep the capers and parsley. This way, everything is ready to be tossed together as soon as you pull the pan from the oven. After the sizzle fades, the tangy, briny, herbal flavors will work their way into the nooks and crannies of the florets.

1 Preheat the oven to 425°F (220°C or gas mark 7).

2 Spread the cauliflower between two rimmed baking sheets, drizzle with the oil, sprinkle with a pinch of salt and the red pepper flakes, and toss to coat. Spread in an even layer. Roast until lightly browned, tossing once halfway through, about 30 minutes total. Once out of the oven, add 2 tablespoons (30 ml) of the Lemon-Caper Dressing, parsley, capers, and raisins to the hot baking sheet and toss with the cauliflower.

3 Meanwhile, cook the orzo according to the package instructions and drain well.

4 To serve, divide the kidney beans among four bowls. Top with the orzo, cauliflower mixture, and steamed spinach. Drizzle with the remaining dressing and garnish with the pine nuts and additional parsley.

Serves 4

1 small head white cauliflower (1 to 1½ pounds [455 to 680 g]), cut into bite-size pieces

1 small head purple cauliflower (1 to 1½ pounds [455 to 680 g]), cut into bite-size pieces

2 tablespoons (30 ml) extra virgin olive oil

Kosher salt

¼ teaspoon red pepper flakes

1 recipe Lemon-Caper Dressing (page 18), divided

¼ cup (15 g) chopped fresh parsley leaves, plus more for topping

2 tablespoons (16 g) capers, drained and roughly chopped

2 tablespoons (16 g) golden raisins

½ cup ((60 g) dried orzo

3 cups (720 ml) or 2 (15-ounce [420 g]) cans kidney beans, drained and rinsed

10 ounces (280 g) baby spinach, steamed

⅓ cup (45 g) toasted pine nuts

Spiced Red Lentil Bowls

This bowl was born shortly after my husband's friend gifted us a batch of his family's signature berbere spice blend. It's an Ethiopian spice blend with a fiery red hue that typically combines fenugreek, cardamom, cumin, chile, ginger, paprika, and more to deliver a warm aroma that's spicy, sweet, and bitter. The combination and amount of each spice can vary from blend to blend, giving each one subtle nuance, and some (like ours!) can really pack in the heat more than others. Start with 1 tablespoon (8 g) of the mix; if it's on the mild side, go ahead and add a second tablespoon (8 g) the next time you make this bowl. Tangy pickled fennel, along with cauliflower rice, earthy chard, and fresh cilantro, are a nice balance to the warm blend of spices.

Serves 4

3 tablespoons (45 ml) avocado or
  extra virgin olive oil, divided
1 medium onion, diced
2 cloves garlic, grated
1-inch (2.5 cm) piece fresh ginger,
  peeled and finely grated
2 tablespoons (30 g) tomato paste
1 tablespoon (8 g) berbere, plus
  more as desired
1 teaspoon ground coriander
Kosher salt and freshly ground
  black pepper
1 cup (190 g) red lentils
4 cups (960 ml) low-sodium
  vegetable broth
1 cup (240 ml) canned unsweetened
  coconut milk
1 pound (455 g) cauliflower rice
1 bunch red chard, leaves and stems
  chopped
1 small fennel bulb, thinly sliced
  and pickled (page 25)
¼ cup (4 g) chopped fresh cilantro
  leaves and tender stems

1 Heat 1 tablespoon (15 ml) of the oil in a Dutch oven or large pot over medium heat until shimmering. Add the onion and sauté until softened, about 5 minutes. Stir in the garlic, ginger, tomato paste, berbere, coriander, a pinch of salt, and a few grinds of pepper and cook until fragrant, 1 to 2 minutes. Add the lentils, broth, and coconut milk and stir to combine. Bring to a boil over medium-high heat, then reduce the heat to low and simmer, stirring occasionally, until soft, about 20 minutes.

2 Meanwhile, heat 1 tablespoon (15 ml) of the oil in a large skillet over medium heat. Add the cauliflower rice, season with salt and pepper, and sauté until tender, about 5 minutes. Divide among four bowls.

3 Heat the remaining 1 tablespoon (15 ml) oil in the same skillet over medium heat. Add the chard leaves and stems and sauté until wilted, about 5 minutes.

4 To serve, spoon the lentils over the cauliflower rice and top with the chard, pickled fennel, and fresh cilantro.

Get a head start! | The lentils and red chard can be cooked in advance, stored in separate containers, and reheated before serving.

Summer Bean Bowls

With a mix of French lentils, red kidney beans, green beans, *and* wax beans, this protein-rich bowl could have been named the legume lover's bowl. That might sound like a lot of legumes in one meal, though it's hardly overwhelming. Instead, inspired by my favorite summery lentil salad—which combines crunchy cucumbers, briny olives, creamy avocado, and a mess of fresh herbs—and classic three-bean salad (another summer essential), these bowls are light and fresh, yet totally satisfying. As for the herbs, anything you have on hand will work nicely here.

Serves 4

¾ cup (145 g) French lentils, rinsed

1 clove garlic, peeled and smashed

Kosher salt

8 ounces (225 g) green beans, trimmed and halved

8 ounces (225 g) wax beans, trimmed and halved

2 tablespoons (30 ml) extra virgin olive oil

1 leek, white part only, halved lengthwise and thinly sliced

1½ cups (360 g) or 1 (15-ounce [420 g]) can kidney beans, drained and rinsed

¼ cup (4 to 15 g) finely chopped fresh herbs, such as parsley, basil, tarragon, dill, or a mix

8 ounces (225 g) baby spinach, steamed

½ English cucumber, chopped

⅓ cup (35 g) pitted Niçoise olives

1 recipe Herbed Avocado Sauce (page 14)

1 Place the lentils, garlic, and a pinch of salt in a large saucepan and cover with water by 2 inches (5 cm). Bring to a boil over medium-high heat, then reduce the heat to low and simmer until the lentils are tender, about 25 minutes. Drain, remove and discard the garlic, and set aside. Rinse out the pan to cook the beans.

2 Use the same saucepan to cook the green and wax beans in salted boiling water until crisp-tender, about 2 minutes. Drain and rinse.

3 Heat the oil in a large skillet over medium heat until shimmering. Add the leek and sauté, stirring occasionally, until softened, about 3 minutes. Add the lentils, green beans, wax beans, and kidney beans. Cook, stirring regularly, until heated through, about 2 minutes. Remove from the heat and stir in the herbs.

4 To serve, divide the lentil and bean mixture among four bowls. Top with the steamed spinach, chopped cucumber, and olives. Drizzle with the Herbed Avocado Sauce.

Get a head start! | The lentils, green beans, and wax beans can be cooked a day in advance. When ready to serve, add directly to the skillet with the leeks and add a few extra minutes to the cook time.

Smoky Marinated Lentil Bowls with Roasted Poblanos

What started with inspiration from my favorite plant-based tacos—meaty lentils partnered with strips of roasted poblano pepper and mushrooms—turned into hearty, flavorful bowls that are far greater than the sum of their parts. Marinating the lentils in a mix of zippy lime juice, smoky cumin, sweet red onion, and cilantro infuses them with so much flavor that has a wonderful way of carrying through the rest of the bowl. If there's any leftover marinade in the bottom of the bowl, I strongly recommend either drizzling it over the bowls or blending it into the cashew sauce.

1 Place the lime juice, 1 tablespoon (15 ml) of the oil, cumin, a pinch of salt, and a few grinds of black pepper in a large bowl and whisk to combine. Add the lentils, red onion, and cilantro. Stir to coat and marinate for at least 30 minutes.

2 Meanwhile, preheat the oven to 400°F (200°C or gas mark 6). Place the poblanos and mushrooms on a rimmed baking sheet, drizzle with the remaining 1 tablespoon (15 ml) oil, and toss to coat. Roast until tender, 12 to 15 minutes.

3 To serve, divide the rainbow chard among four bowls. Top with the marinated lentil mixture, roasted poblano peppers and mushrooms, and radish. Drizzle with the Creamy Herb Sauce and sprinkle with the sunflower seeds.

Get a head start! | The lentils should be marinated for at least 30 minutes but can be marinated a day in advance and stored in an airtight container in the refrigerator until serving.

Serves 4

Juice from 2 limes

2 tablespoons (30 ml) extra virgin olive oil, divided

1 teaspoon ground cumin

Kosher salt and freshly ground black pepper

1½ cups (300 g) cooked brown lentils

½ small red onion, thinly sliced

½ cup (8 g) chopped fresh cilantro leaves and tender stems

2 poblano peppers, halved and seeded

2 portobello mushrooms, cut into ½-inch (1.3 cm)-thick slices

1 small bunch rainbow chard, stems removed and leaves thinly sliced

1 medium watermelon radish, thinly sliced

1 recipe Creamy Herb Sauce made with cilantro (page 15)

⅓ cup (45 g) unsalted toasted sunflower seeds

NOODLE
BOOWLS

Roasted Vegetable and Kohlrabi Noodle Bowls with Peanut Sauce

You can never go wrong with peanut noodle bowls piled high with veggies. In fact, it's usually my default dinner when I can't decide what to cook. I grab whatever vegetables are lingering in the crisper, and while they're roasting in the oven, I stir together a quick batch of peanut sauce. And when I want to change it up (and pack in more veggies), I swap my usual soba or rice noodles for kohlrabi noodles. Kohlrabi is a totally underrated vegetable with a mild-mannered taste and a crisp texture akin to broccoli stalks or an extra-firm apple, which makes it perfect for spiralizing into noodles.

1 Preheat the oven to 425°F (220°C or gas mark 7). Line a baking sheet with parchment paper.

2 Place the tofu on the prepared baking sheet, drizzle with 2 tablespoons (30 ml) of the Peanut Sauce and the soy sauce, sprinkle with a pinch of salt and a few grinds of black pepper, and toss to coat. Roast for 15 minutes, flip the tofu, and cook for 15 minutes longer.

3 Meanwhile, add the broccolini and sliced carrots to a second rimmed baking sheet, drizzle with the oil, season with salt and a few grinds of black pepper, and toss to coat. Arrange the vegetables in a single layer and roast for 15 minutes.

4 To serve, divide the kohlrabi noodles and chopped basil among four bowls and toss to combine. Top with the broccolini, carrots, and edamame; drizzle with the remaining Peanut Sauce; and garnish with the scallions, chopped peanuts, and coconut flakes.

Get a head start! | The broccolini and carrots can be roasted a day in advance and reheated before serving.

Serves 4

14 ounces (392 g) extra-firm tofu, drained, pressed, and torn into bite-size pieces

1 recipe Peanut Sauce (page 21), divided

1 tablespoon (15 ml) soy sauce or tamari

Kosher salt and freshly ground black pepper

2 small bunches broccolini (about 1 pound [455 g]), ends trimmed

1 pound (455 g) rainbow carrots, peeled and sliced on the diagonal into ¼-inch (6 mm)-thick pieces

2 tablespoons (30 ml) avocado or extra virgin olive oil

1½ pounds (680 g) kohlrabi, peeled and spiralized

½ cup (30 g) chopped fresh basil leaves

1 cup (150 g) shelled edamame, thawed if frozen

2 scallions, thinly sliced

¼ cup (35 g) chopped unsalted roasted peanuts

¼ cup (20 g) unsweetened toasted coconut flakes

Summer Roll Noodle Bowls

Piled high inside this bowl is everything there is to love about super fresh summer rolls, from the mix of greens and fresh herbs to the sweet carrot, bell pepper, cucumber, and creamy avocado. Plus, protein-rich shelled edamame and a drizzle of Peanut Sauce keep it satisfying.

Serves 4

6 ounces (168 g) vermicelli rice
    noodles
1 teaspoon toasted sesame oil
2 cups (60 g) mixed greens
¼ cup (15 g) roughly chopped fresh
    basil leaves, plus more for serving
¼ cup (15 g) roughly chopped fresh
    mint leaves, plus more for serving
1 cup (150 g) shelled edamame,
    thawed if frozen
2 medium carrots, peeled and shaved
2 Persian cucumbers, thinly sliced
1 medium red bell pepper, cored,
    seeded, and thinly sliced
2 avocados, peeled, pitted, and
    halved
1 recipe Peanut Sauce (page 21)
1 tablespoon (8 g) toasted
    sesame seeds
1 lime, quartered, for serving

1 Cook the rice noodles according to the package instructions. Drain, place in a bowl, and toss with the sesame oil. In another bowl, toss the greens and herbs together.

2 To serve, divide the greens among four bowls. Top with the rice noodles, followed by the edamame, carrot, cucumber, bell pepper, and avocado. Drizzle with the Peanut Sauce and garnish with the sesame seeds, a lime wedge, and additional herbs, if desired.

Crispy Kale and Tahini Soba Noodle Bowls

I'll let you decide whether the star of this noodle bowl is the pile of lemony, pepper-kissed kale chips or the toasted chickpeas. For me, it's definitely those kale leaves that crumble into pieces when you bite into them. While I generally prefer Tuscan kale, purple kale (or even curly green kale) is the best choice for quickly toasting under the broiler because all of the curly edges mean more crunch.

1 Cook the soba noodles according to the package instructions. Drain and rinse well with cool water. Add to a large bowl and toss with ½ cup (120 ml) of the Lemon Tahini Sauce and the sesame seeds.

2 Meanwhile, arrange a rack at least 6 inches (15 cm) under the broiler and heat the oven to broil. Place the kale leaves and chickpeas on a rimmed baking sheet. Drizzle with the olive oil and lemon juice, sprinkle with a pinch of salt and red pepper flakes, and toss to coat. Broil until the kale is crispy, about 5 minutes.

3 To serve, divide the noodles among four bowls. Top with the kale and chickpea mixture, carrots, and pickled radishes. Drizzle with the remaining sauce and garnish with the Savory Seed Sprinkle.

Serves 4

8 ounces (225 g) dried buckwheat soba noodles

1 recipe Lemon Tahini Sauce (page 18), divided

1 tablespoon (8 g) toasted sesame seeds

1 bunch purple kale (about 10 ounces [280 g]), stems and center ribs removed and leaves torn

1½ cups (360 g) or 1 (15-ounce [420 g]) can chickpeas, drained and rinsed

3 tablespoons (45 ml) extra virgin olive oil

Juice from ½ lemon

Kosher salt

Pinch of red pepper flakes

2 medium carrots, peeled and thinly shaved

1 bunch radishes, thinly sliced and pickled (page 25)

⅓ cup (45 g) Savory Seed Sprinkle (page 16)

Kale Pesto Soba Noodle Bowls

Anytime you have a big bunch of kale that's on its last legs and needs to get used up sooner than later, turn it into a bright green pesto and slather it all over a bowl of nutty soba noodles. You won't regret it, trust me. Not only is it a good strategy for using up some kale, but it's also a fun way to change up your regular noodle bowl routine. White beans keep the bowls filling, while fermented kraut adds a punchy twist (and some probiotics!).

Serves 4

1½ pounds (680 g) golden beets, red beets, or a combination, peeled and cut into ½-inch (1.3 cm) cubes
8 ounces (225 g) dried buckwheat soba noodles
1½ cups (360 g) or 1 (15-ounce [420 g]) can cannellini beans
1 recipe Kale-Almond Pesto Sauce (page 19), divided
1½ cups (360 g) fermented red cabbage kraut
¼ cup (35 g) Hazelnut Dukkah (page 24)

1 Place the cubed beets in a steamer basket fitted in a large saucepan, with 2 inches (5 cm) of water at the bottom. Cover and steam until tender, about 20 minutes.

2 Meanwhile, cook the soba noodles according to the package instructions. Drain, without rinsing, and return the noodles to the pot. Add the beans and ½ cup (120 ml) of the Kale-Almond Pesto Sauce, and toss to combine.

3 To serve, divide the soba noodles and beans among four bowls. Top with the beets, red cabbage kraut, and the remaining pesto and sprinkle with the Hazelnut Dukkah.

> **Get a head start!** | The beets and sauce can be made a day in advance and stored in separate containers in the refrigerator until serving.

Eggplant and Mushroom Soba Noodle Bowls

Fairy tale eggplant is proof that really great things come in small packages. These palm-size eggplants show up at the farmers' market in mid- to late summer, and their time is fleeting, so don't delay in buying a basket or two when you spot them. Unlike larger globe eggplant that can be tough or mealy, these are quite the opposite. Here, they're halved lengthwise and seared face-down in a hot skillet until beautifully caramelized with creamy flesh, then kissed with a shower of fresh garlic and ginger. If you can't find fairy tale eggplant, Japanese eggplant makes a nice substitute.

Serves 4

3 tablespoons (45 ml) avocado or
    extra virgin olive oil, divided
8 ounces (225 g) mixed mushrooms,
    such as cremini, shiitake,
    and oyster
Kosher salt and freshly ground
    black pepper
1 pound (455 g) fairy tale eggplant,
    halved lengthwise, or Japanese
    eggplant, cut into ½-inch
    (1.3 cm)-thick rounds
2 cloves garlic, minced
2 teaspoons chopped fresh ginger
1 tablespoon (15 ml) soy sauce
    or tamari
6 ounces (168 g) dried buckwheat
    soba noodles
2 cups (140 g) finely shredded
    red cabbage
2 tablespoons (16 g) hemp seeds,
    plus more for topping
1 recipe Green Tahini Sauce
    (page 22), divided
1 cup (150 g) shelled edamame,
    thawed if frozen
½ cup (30 g) chopped fresh basil
    leaves

1 Heat 1 tablespoon (15 ml) of the oil in a large skillet over medium-high heat until shimmering. Add the mushrooms and cook, undisturbed in a single layer, until lightly browned on the bottom, about 4 minutes. Toss and cook for 3 minutes longer. Transfer to a plate and sprinkle with a pinch of salt.

2 Heat the remaining 2 tablespoons (30 ml) oil in the same skillet over medium-high heat until shimmering. Add the eggplant cut-side down and cook until lightly browned, 4 to 5 minutes. Flip with tongs; add the garlic, ginger, and soy sauce; season with salt and a few grinds of black pepper; and cook for 2 minutes longer.

3 Cook the soba noodles according to the package instructions. Drain, without rinsing; return the noodles to the pot; add the cabbage and hemp seeds; and toss with about ⅓ cup (80 ml) of the Green Tahini Sauce.

4 To serve, divide the noodles and cabbage among four bowls. Top with the mushrooms, eggplant, and edamame. Drizzle with the remaining sauce and sprinkle with the fresh basil and more hemp seeds.

Miso Noodle Bowls with Tempeh Crumbles

Bok choy is a great option if you're looking to change up your greens game. While it's low in calories, it's packed with vitamins, notably vitamins C and E, as well as folate, and it's just as much a star in this bowl as the punchy miso-coated noodles. You'll quickly wilt the chopped greens in a wok or large skillet before tossing in the noodles and about half of the sauce. Just remember to drain and rinse the noodles first, so they don't clump together.

1 Steam the block of tempeh in a large saucepan fitted with a steamer basket for 10 minutes. Pat dry. When cool enough to handle, crumble into small pieces.

2 Use the same saucepan to cook the noodles according to the package instructions. Drain, rinse well with cool water, and set aside.

3 Meanwhile, heat 1½ tablespoons (23 ml) of the oil in a wok or large skillet over medium-high heat until shimmering. Add the tempeh and cook, stirring often, until lightly browned and crisp, 5 to 7 minutes. Transfer to a plate; set aside.

4 Heat the remaining 1 tablespoon (15 ml) oil in the wok or skillet over medium heat. Add the bok choy and a pinch of salt. Cook, tossing regularly, until wilted, 1 to 2 minutes. Add the noodles, toss together, and cook for 1 minute longer. Remove from the heat and stir in ⅓ cup (80 ml) of the Miso-Ginger Sauce.

5 To serve, divide the noodles and bok choy among four bowls. Top with the reserved tempeh, carrots, and snap peas. Drizzle with the remaining sauce and sprinkle with the cashews.

Serves 4

8 ounces (225 g) tempeh

8 ounces (225 g) vegan ramen noodles

2½ tablespoons (37 ml) avocado or extra virgin olive oil, divided

1 medium head bok choy, trimmed and chopped

Kosher salt

1 recipe Miso-Ginger Sauce (page 20), divided

1 cup (110 g) shredded carrot

8 ounces (225 g) snap peas, halved lengthwise

¼ cup (35 g) chopped unsalted toasted cashews

Orange-Sesame Noodle Bowls

by classic sesame noodles, this noodle bowl gets extra flavor from freshly squeezed ice and a pinch of coriander, and goes all in on the greens with tender asparagus, kale, mame. Finishing the bowl with a shower of fresh herbs is optional, though I can never dding lots of fresh cilantro.

the orange juice, soy sauce, maple syrup, cornstarch, oil, garlic, coriander, red pepper flakes, and a pinch of salt dium bowl and whisk well until the cornstarch is dissolved. le.

the noodles according to the package instructions. nd rinse well.

at the oil in a wok or large skillet over medium-high heat until shimmering. Add the noodles and kale, and stir-fry, tossing constantly, until heated through, about 1 minute. Whisk the sauce to recombine and add to the pan along with the sesame seeds. Toss until the sauce evenly coats the noodles and is slightly thickened, about 1 minute.

4 To serve, divide the noodles among four bowls. Top with the asparagus, edamame, and scallions and sprinkle with additional sesame seeds and fresh herbs.

Serves 4

⅓ cup (80 ml) freshly squeezed orange juice

¼ cup (60 ml) soy sauce or tamari

1 tablespoon (15 ml) pure maple syrup

2 teaspoons cornstarch

1 teaspoon toasted sesame oil

2 cloves garlic, grated

½ teaspoon ground coriander

Pinch of red pepper flakes

Kosher salt

8 ounces (225 g) dry wide rice noodles

1 tablespoon (15 ml) avocado or extra virgin olive oil

1 small bunch Tuscan kale, leaves finely shredded

1 tablespoon (8 g) toasted black sesame seeds, plus more for topping

1 bunch asparagus, trimmed, halved, and steamed

2 cups (300 g) shelled edamame, thawed if frozen

2 scallions, thinly sliced on the diagonal

Chopped fresh herbs, such as cilantro, basil, or mint (optional)

Sweet Potato Noodle Bowls with Ginger Peanut Broth

If you have a thing for peanut noodles, these wholesome bowls will be right up your alley. After being infused with garlic and ginger, the broth is thickened with peanut butter, which lands it in my favorite place—somewhere between brothy and super saucy. The thick broth expertly coats the sweet potato noodles and crispy cubes of tofu and gives these otherwise light and fresh bowls a hint of richness.

Serves 4

14 ounces (392 g) extra-firm tofu, drained, pressed, and cut into 1-inch (2.5 cm) cubes
1 tablespoon (15 ml) virgin coconut oil
1 tablespoon (8 g) cornstarch
Kosher salt and freshly ground black pepper
3 cups (720 ml) low-sodium vegetable broth
2 tablespoons (16 g) chopped fresh ginger
2 cloves garlic, thinly sliced
¼ cup (60 g) natural creamy peanut butter
1 pound (455 g) sweet potato noodles
4 ounces (112 g) snow peas, halved
6 radishes, thinly sliced
¼ cup (35 g) unsalted roasted peanuts

1 Preheat the oven to 400ºF (200ºC or gas mark 6). Line a baking sheet with parchment paper.

2 Place the tofu in a large bowl, drizzle with the coconut oil, and toss to coat. Sprinkle with the cornstarch, a pinch of salt, and a few grinds of black pepper and toss to coat again. Spread in a single layer on the prepared baking sheet. Bake for 20 minutes.

3 Meanwhile, combine the vegetable broth, ginger, and garlic in a large saucepan and simmer for 15 minutes. Remove from the heat, add the peanut butter, and stir until completely dissolved. Add the sweet potato noodles to the warm broth, cover, and let sit until the noodles are barely tender, about 5 minutes.

4 To serve, divide the sweet potato noodles and broth among four bowls. Top with the baked tofu, snow peas, and radishes and sprinkle with the peanuts.

Satay Noodle Bowls

This bright and fresh bowl is as much about the rich and creamy coconut-spiked sauce as it is about the noodles and toppings. It starts with a satay-inspired peanut sauce that's mixed with a touch of coconut milk and heated on the stove until thin and creamy, with just a hint of decadence. After you drain the rice noodles, toss them back in the pot with a few spoonfuls of the sauce—they'll soak up just enough to infuse them with plenty of nutty flavor.

1 Preheat the oven to 400°F (200°C or gas mark 6). Line a baking sheet with parchment paper.

2 Arrange the tofu in a single layer on the prepared baking sheet and sprinkle with salt and a few grinds of black pepper. Bake until dried out and lightly browned, stirring once halfway through, 30 minutes total. Place the tofu in a bowl with ¼ cup (60 ml) of the Satay Peanut Sauce and gently stir to coat.

3 Meanwhile, prepare the noodles according to the package instructions. Drain, place in a bowl, and toss with a few spoonfuls of the peanut sauce.

4 To serve, divide the noodles among four bowls. Top with the tofu, cucumber, and edamame; drizzle with the remaining sauce; and sprinkle with the coconut flakes, mint leaves, and red pepper flakes.

Serves 4

14 ounces (392 g) extra-firm tofu, drained, pressed, and cubed
Kosher salt and freshly ground black pepper
1 recipe Satay Peanut Sauce (page 21), divided
8 ounces (225 g) dry wide rice noodles
3 Persian cucumbers, chopped
1½ cups (225 g) shelled edamame, thawed if frozen
⅓ cup (28 g) unsweetened toasted coconut flakes
¼ cup (15 g) chopped fresh mint leaves
Red pepper flakes

Spicy Red Curry Noodle Bowls

Unlike brothy red curries where the vegetables simmer in the pot until they're melt-in-your-mouth soft, these bowls dial back the broth and load up on the noodles and roasted vegetables. Roasting keeps the broccoli and zucchini tender and toothsome, with the warm char you can only get from a hot oven. And while the bowls aren't brothy, there's still plenty of sauce, so you'll get a taste with every bite. Don't worry too much about being exact when measuring the cilantro. I like to think of it here more as a leafy green than a garnish.

Serves 4

1 medium head broccoli, cut into bite-size florets

2 medium zucchini, halved lengthwise and sliced

3 tablespoons (45 ml) virgin coconut oil, divided

Kosher salt and freshly ground black pepper

8 ounces (225 g) dry wide rice noodles

2 cloves garlic, minced

1-inch (2.5 cm) piece fresh ginger, peeled and finely grated

3 tablespoons (45 g) vegan Thai red curry paste

1 (14-ounce [392 g]) can unsweetened full-fat coconut milk

½ cup (120 ml) low-sodium vegetable broth

2 tablespoons (30 ml) soy sauce or tamari

1 tablespoon (15 ml) agave nectar

1 tablespoon (15 ml) freshly squeezed lime juice

1 cup (50 g) bean sprouts

3 scallions, thinly sliced

½ bunch fresh cilantro leaves, roughly chopped

1 Preheat the oven to 400ºF (200ºC or gas mark 6).

2 Place the broccoli florets and sliced zucchini on a rimmed baking sheet, drizzle with 2 tablespoons (30 ml) of the coconut oil, and season with salt and pepper. Roast until tender and lightly browned, flipping once halfway through, about 20 minutes total.

3 Meanwhile, cook the rice noodles according to the package instructions. Drain and rinse well.

4 Heat the remaining 1 tablespoon (15 ml) coconut oil in a large, high-sided skillet over medium heat. Add the garlic and ginger and cook until fragrant, about 30 seconds. Stir in the curry paste and cook for 2 minutes longer. Stir in the coconut milk and broth and season with salt and a few grinds of black pepper. Bring to a boil over medium-high heat, then reduce the heat to low and simmer until slightly thickened, about 10 minutes. Stir in the soy sauce, agave, and lime juice. Add the noodles and toss to coat.

5 To serve, divide the noodles among four bowls. Top with the roasted broccoli and zucchini, bean sprouts, sliced scallion, and fresh cilantro, and spoon the sauce over the top.

Get a head start! | The broccoli and zucchini can be roasted a day in advance and reheated before serving.

Stir-Fried Celery Bowls with Soba Noodles and Spicy Peanut Sauce

Consider this crunchy stir-fry bowl your friendly reminder that celery is so much more than a filler vegetable or something to leave in the fridge as an emergency snack. It happens to be one of my favorite vegetables to stir-fry, because just a minute or two in a hot skillet tames the flavor and leaves it with a tender-crisp texture. You'll start with a full head of celery—the stalks all get stir-fried and the leaves are mixed in at the end, along with fresh basil and toasted cashews.

1 Cook the soba noodles according to the package instructions. Drain and set aside.

2 Heat 2 tablespoons (30 ml) of the oil in a wok or large skillet over medium-high heat until very hot but not smoking. Add the mushrooms, season with a pinch of salt and freshly ground black pepper, and stir-fry until tender and crispy around the edges, 5 minutes. Transfer to a plate and set aside.

3 Heat the remaining 1 tablespoon (15 ml) oil in the same wok or skillet over medium-high heat. Add the sliced celery, snow peas, and scallions and season with a pinch of salt and pepper. Stir-fry for 2 minutes. Return the mushrooms to the pan, add the ginger and about ¼ cup (60 ml) of the Spicy Peanut Sauce, and cook for 1 minute longer. Remove from the heat and mix in the celery leaves, cashews, and basil.

4 To serve, divide the noodles among four bowls. Top with the stir-fried vegetables. Drizzle with the remaining sauce and garnish with additional basil, if desired.

Serves 4

8 ounces (225 g) dry buckwheat soba noodles

3 tablespoons (45 ml) avocado oil, divided

8 ounces (225 g) shiitake mushrooms, sliced

Kosher salt and freshly ground black pepper

1 head celery, stalks trimmed and cut on the diagonal into ½-inch (1.3 cm)-thick slices, leaves reserved

4 ounces (112 g) snow peas

1 bunch scallions, trimmed and sliced into 2-inch (5 cm) pieces

1-inch (2.5 cm) piece fresh ginger, peeled and julienned

1 recipe Spicy Peanut Sauce (page 21), divided

⅓ cup (45 g) chopped unsalted toasted cashews

¼ cup (15 g) chopped fresh basil leaves, plus more for garnish, if desired

HUMMUS
BOWLS

Mushroom Shawarma Bowls

A mix of meaty mushrooms make the perfect stand-in for otherwise meat-heavy shawarma. They're coated with a blend of warm, smoky spices, like cumin, paprika, turmeric, and a pinch of cinnamon, plus a squeeze of lemon, before being roasted until perfectly tender with lightly crisped edges. A blanket of creamy hummus takes the place of sauce, though if you can't resist a drizzle of something extra over the top, try the Green Tahini Sauce (page 22) for something bright and nutty or the Chimichurri Sauce (page 12) for a finish that's super herby and punchy.

Serves 4

1 tablespoon (6 g) ground cumin
2 teaspoons sweet paprika
½ teaspoon ground turmeric
¼ teaspoon ground cinnamon
Kosher salt and freshly ground
    black pepper
Pinch of cayenne pepper
4 portobello mushroom caps, cut
    into ½-inch (1.3 cm)-thick slices
    and halved
8 ounces (225 g) oyster mushrooms
2 tablespoons (30 ml) extra virgin
    olive oil
2 tablespoons (30 ml) freshly
    squeezed lemon juice
2 plum tomatoes, halved
1 recipe Creamy Hummus (page 17)
4 packed cups (120 g) chopped
    romaine
4 radishes, julienned
1 small red onion, thinly sliced and
    pickled (page 25)

1 Preheat the oven to 400ºF (200ºC or gas mark 6).

2 Mix together the cumin, paprika, turmeric, cinnamon, ½ teaspoon salt, ¼ teaspoon black pepper, and cayenne pepper in a small bowl. Add the mushrooms to a rimmed baking sheet, drizzle with the oil and lemon juice, sprinkle with the spice mixture, and toss to coat. Arrange in an even layer and place the tomatoes cut-side up on the baking sheet. Roast until softened, about 15 minutes.

3 To serve, spread the Creamy Hummus over the bottom of four bowls. Top with the chopped romaine, roasted tomatoes, mushrooms, radishes, and pickled onion.

Za'atar Roasted Vegetable Bowls

Do you ever have those nights when you just want to eat a pile of roasted vegetables for dinner? I know I do. Here's how to do it, and have a meal that's not just wholesome and nourishing, but also really satisfying and filling. A sprinkle of za'atar—the Middle Eastern spice blend with a mix of dried thyme, sumac, and sesame seeds—plus a squeeze of lime juice just before serving, livens up basic roasted vegetables with hints of herbal, nutty flavor with a little smokiness and a pop of tang.

Serves 4

1 small head cauliflower (about 1½ pounds [680 g]), cut into bite-size florets
1 pound (455 g) Brussels sprouts, trimmed and halved
1 large sweet potato (about 1 pound [455 g]), peeled and cubed
2 tablespoons (30 ml) extra virgin olive oil
2 tablespoons (12 g) za'atar
Kosher salt and freshly ground black pepper
1 recipe Creamy Hummus (page 17)
2 packed cups (60 g) arugula
¼ cup (4 g) chopped fresh cilantro leaves and tender stems
¼ cup (35 g) chopped toasted hazelnuts
1 lime, quartered
Warm pita, for serving (optional)

1 Preheat the oven to 400ºF (200ºC or gas mark 6).

2 In a large bowl, toss the cauliflower, Brussels sprouts, and sweet potato with the oil, za'atar, a pinch of salt, and a few grinds of black pepper. Arrange on two rimmed baking sheets in a single layer. Roast until tender and lightly browned, tossing once halfway through, about 30 minutes total.

3 To serve, spread the Creamy Hummus over the bottom of four bowls. Top with the arugula and roasted vegetables, sprinkle with the cilantro and chopped hazelnuts, and finish with a squeeze of lime. Serve with warm pita, if desired.

Smoky Butternut Squash Hummus Bowls

I used to think that there was no better way to eat butternut squash than when it was roasted until the center was tender and the edges caramelized and slightly crisp. That changed entirely the first time I blitzed butternut squash into "hummus." This smooth dip gets a rich and nutty flavor from the tahini, plus a squeeze of lemon and pinch of smoky spices. If you can't find Romanesco—a cousin to cauliflower—grab a small head of cauliflower instead. A wedge or two of warm pita for serving is optional, though always a must for me.

1 Preheat the oven to 400°F (200°C or gas mark 6).

2 In a large bowl, toss the Romanesco, onion, and beans with the oil, a pinch of salt, and a few grinds of black pepper and arrange in a single layer on a rimmed baking sheet. Roast until tender and lightly brown, tossing once halfway through, about 25 minutes total.

3 Meanwhile, steam the butternut squash and let cool slightly.

4 Place the cooled butternut squash, tahini, lemon juice, garlic, smoked paprika, cumin, a pinch of salt, and a few grinds of black pepper in a food processor or blender. Process until smooth and creamy, scraping down the sides as necessary.

5 To serve, spread the butternut squash hummus over the bottom of four bowls. Top with the arugula, roasted vegetables and beans, pomegranate arils, and cilantro. If desired, serve with warm pita bread.

Get a head start! | The hummus can be made a day in advance and stored in an airtight container in the refrigerator. The Romanesco, onion, and beans can be roasted a day in advance and reheated before serving.

Serves 4

1 head Romanesco, cut into bite-size florets

1 large red onion, halved and sliced into thick strips

1½ cups (360 g) or 1 (15-ounce [420 g]) can cannellini beans, drained and rinsed

2 tablespoons (30 ml) avocado or extra virgin olive oil

Kosher salt and freshly ground black pepper

1½ pounds (680 g) cubed butternut squash

½ cup (120 g) tahini

Juice from 1 lemon

1 clove garlic

½ teaspoon smoked paprika

½ teaspoon ground cumin

5 ounces (140 g) arugula

¼ cup (35 g) pomegranate arils

¼ cup (4 g) chopped fresh cilantro leaves

Warm pita, for serving (optional)

Roasted Beet Hummus Bowls

I know looks aren't everything, but just *look* at this beet hummus. It's a total stunner, and it has the most irresistible taste to match. Here, white beans are blended with earthy steamed beetroot. Make it a meal by rounding out your bowl with toothsome black lentils (if you can't find them, French lentils make a nice substitute), sautéed shredded kale and Brussels sprouts, and crisp cucumber.

1 Preheat the oven to 400ºF (200ºC or gas mark 6).

2 Wrap the beetroot in foil and roast until tender enough to be pierced through with a knife, 60 to 70 minutes. When cool enough to handle, use a paper towel to rub off the beet skin and discard. Remove the root and roughly chop the beet.

3 Place the chopped beet, white beans, tahini, lemon juice, garlic, fennel seed, a pinch of salt, and a few grinds of black pepper in a food processor or blender. Process until smooth and creamy.

4 Place the lentils and a pinch of salt in a medium saucepan and cover with water by at least 2 inches (5 cm). Bring to a boil over medium-high heat, then reduce the heat to low, cover, and simmer until tender, about 25 minutes. Drain the excess water.

5 Meanwhile, heat the oil in a large skillet over medium heat until shimmering. Add the kale and Brussels sprouts and cook, tossing occasionally, until just wilted, about 3 minutes. Remove from the heat and stir in the carrot.

6 To serve, divide the beet hummus among four bowls and spread over the bottom and up one side. Top with the lentils, kale mixture, cucumber, and pickled fennel and sprinkle with the Savory Seed Sprinkle. Serve with warm pita, if desired.

Serves 4

1 medium red beet (about 6 ounces [168 g])

1½ cups (360 g) or 1 (15-ounce [420 g]) can white beans, drained and rinsed

⅓ cup (80 g) tahini

Juice from 1 lemon

1 clove garlic

½ teaspoon fennel seed

Kosher salt and freshly ground black pepper

¾ cup (140 g) black beluga lentils, rinsed

1½ tablespoons (23 ml) avocado or extra virgin olive oil

1 small bunch Tuscan kale, leaves thinly shredded

8 ounces (225 g) Brussels sprouts, trimmed and shredded

½ cup (55 g) shredded rainbow carrot

2 Persian cucumbers, chopped

1 medium fennel bulb, thinly sliced and pickled (page 25)

2 tablespoons (16 g) Savory Seed Sprinkle (page 16)

Warm pita, for serving (optional)

Get a head start! | The beetroot can be roasted, peeled, and chopped a day ahead and stored in the refrigerator. The hummus can be made a day in advance and stored in an airtight container in the refrigerator. The lentils can be cooked in advance and reheated, if desired, before serving.

Loaded Falafel Bowls

There's a restaurant near my apartment with the best falafel wraps I've ever tasted. What makes them so great is the way all the crunchy, creamy, tangy add-ins play with the spiced falafel, and they serve as the inspiration for these bowls. The baked falafel patties are loaded with warm spices and fresh herbs.

Serves 4

1 (15-ounce) can chickpeas, drained and rinsed, OR 1 cup (200 g) dried chickpeas, soaked in water overnight
1 shallot, roughly chopped
3 cloves garlic
⅓ packed cup (20 g) fresh parsley or cilantro leaves
1 tablespoon (15 ml) freshly squeezed lemon juice
1 teaspoon ground cumin
1 teaspoon ground coriander
Kosher salt and freshly ground black pepper
¼ cup (30 g) all-purpose flour
1 tablespoon (15 ml) plus 1 teaspoon (5 ml) avocado or extra virgin olive oil, divided
6 medium carrots, peeled and cut into ½-inch (1.3 cm)-thick slices
1 recipe Creamy Hummus (page 17)
½ English cucumber, chopped
4 radishes, chopped
½ cup (75 g) grape tomatoes, halved
8 pepperoncini, thinly sliced
½ cup (120 g) fermented red cabbage kraut
Warm pita, for serving (optional)

1 Preheat the oven to 375°F (190°C or gas mark 5).

2 Add the drained chickpeas, shallot, garlic, parsley, lemon juice, cumin, coriander, 1 teaspoon kosher salt, and ¼ teaspoon black pepper to the bowl of a food processor fitted with the blade attachment. Pulse about 10 times until the chickpeas are chopped and the mixture is combined. Scrape down the sides of the bowl, sprinkle in the flour, and pulse until the mixture is well combined.

3 Brush 1 teaspoon (5 ml) of the oil over a rimmed baking sheet. Scoop out about 2 tablespoons (30 g) of the mixture and roll into a ball in the palm of your hands. Transfer to the baking sheet and flatten into a ½-inch (1.3 cm)-thick disk with a spatula. Repeat with the remainder of the mixture. You should have 12 falafel total.

4 Place the carrots on a separate baking sheet, drizzle with the remaining 1 tablespoon (15 ml) oil, and season with salt and pepper. Bake the falafel until cooked through and tender and the carrots are lightly browned, flipping once halfway through, 25 to 30 minutes total.

5 To serve, divide the hummus among four bowls and spread over the bottom of the bowls. Top with three falafel patties per bowl, roasted carrots, chopped cucumber, radishes, pepperoncini, and cabbage kraut and serve with warm pita, if desired.

Spiced Kidney Bean Hummus Bowls

The most fun thing about making your own hummus is changing it up with different beans and seasonings. This version swaps the chickpeas for hearty kidney beans and gets a hint of warm, spiced aroma from garam masala. Kidney beans have a relatively thick skin, so be sure not to skimp on the blending.

1 Place the millet, water, and a pinch of salt in a large saucepan. Bring to a boil over medium-high heat, then reduce the heat to low, cover, and simmer until tender and the water is absorbed, 15 to 20 minutes. Remove from the heat, stir in the spinach, and steam in the pot for 5 minutes. Fluff the millet with a fork.

2 Meanwhile, place the kidney beans, tahini, garlic, water, olive oil, lemon juice, garam masala, and 1 teaspoon kosher salt in the bowl of a food processor fitted with the blade attachment. Process until smooth and creamy, scraping down the sides as necessary. For a thinner consistency, add more water, 1 tablespoon (15 ml) at a time, while the machine is running.

3 To serve, divide the millet among four bowls. Top with the broccolini, hummus, pickled red onion, and warm pita, if desired.

Serves 4

1 cup (160 g) millet
2 cups (480 ml) water
Kosher salt and freshly ground black pepper
2 ounces (56 g) chopped baby spinach
1½ cups (360 g) or 1 (15-ounce [420 g]) can kidney beans, drained and rinsed
¼ cup (60 g) tahini
1 small clove garlic
2 tablespoons (30 ml) water, plus more as needed
2 tablespoons (30 ml) extra virgin olive oil
2 tablespoons (30 ml) lemon juice
1 teaspoon garam masala
2 bunches broccolini, steamed
1 small red onion, thinly sliced and pickled (page 25)
Warm pita, for serving (optional)

Get a head start! | The hummus can be made a day in advance and stored in an airtight container in the refrigerator until ready to serve.

Chipotle Sweet Potato "Hummus" Bowls

These smoky-sweet bowls are inspired by my love for both a luxurious, thick, creamy dip and sweet potatoes. Unlike traditional hummus, there are no chickpeas or beans in this version. Instead it starts with a tender roasted sweet potato that's whipped together with tahini, garlic, lemon, and a pinch of chipotle chili powder, for a lightly spiced, smoky-sweet dip. If you want some extra sauce for topping, try the Avocado Green Goddess Dressing (page 13) or the Chimichurri Sauce (page 12).

Serves 4

1 large sweet potato (about 1 pound [455 g])
1 bunch Tuscan kale, center ribs removed and leaves chopped
1 tablespoon (15 ml) extra virgin olive oil
Juice from 2 lemons, divided
Kosher salt and freshly ground black pepper
¾ cup (125 g) tricolor quinoa, rinsed
⅓ cup (65 g) brown lentils, rinsed
1¾ cups (420 ml) water
½ cup (120 g) tahini
1 clove garlic
½ teaspoon chipotle chile powder
6 mini sweet peppers, cored and thinly sliced
2 avocados, peeled, pitted, and thinly sliced
¼ cup (4 g) chopped fresh cilantro leaves
¼ cup (35 g) toasted pumpkin seeds

1 Preheat the oven to 400ºF (200ºC or gas mark 6).

2 Prick the sweet potato all over with a fork. Place on a baking sheet and roast until tender all the way through, about 1 hour. Set aside until cool enough to handle.

3 Place the kale in a large bowl, drizzle with the oil, the juice from one of the lemons, and a pinch of salt. Massage the kale so it's well coated. Set aside.

4 Place the quinoa, lentils, water, and a pinch of salt in a medium saucepan. Bring to a boil over medium-high heat, then reduce the heat to low, cover, and cook until tender, about 15 minutes. Remove from the heat and keep covered for 5 minutes. Fluff with a fork.

5 Meanwhile, place the cooled sweet potato, juice from the remaining lemon, tahini, garlic, chipotle chile powder, a pinch of salt, and a few grinds of black pepper in a food processor or blender. Process until smooth and creamy, scraping down the sides as necessary.

6 To serve, divide the sweet potato "hummus" among four bowls and spread over the bottom and up one side. Top with the kale, quinoa and lentil mixture, sliced sweet peppers, and avocado. Garnish with the fresh cilantro and toasted pumpkin seeds.

Get a head start! | The sweet potato can be roasted a day in advance and stored in the refrigerator until you blend the hummus, or make the hummus a day in advance and store in an airtight container in the refrigerator. The quinoa and lentil mixture can be made a day in advance and reheated before serving.

Smoky Brussels Sprout Bowls

If roasting is your default for cooking Brussels sprouts, you've got to try this simple stovetop sauté. It's my favorite way to cook Brussels sprouts. The shredded leaves are sautéed until tender and crispy around the edges, and partnered with garlic, smoked paprika, lemon juice, and lemon zest for a flavor that's warm and smoky, yet bright and tangy at the same time.

1 Place the rice and a pinch of salt in a medium saucepan and cover with water by 2 inches (5 cm). Bring to a boil over medium-high heat, then reduce the heat to low and simmer, uncovered, until chewy and some of the grains have burst, 40 to 50 minutes. Drain the excess water.

2 Meanwhile, heat the oil in a large skillet over medium heat until shimmering. Add the shallot and sauté until softened, about 2 minutes. Add the Brussels sprouts, garlic, smoked paprika, lemon zest, a pinch of salt, and a few grinds of black pepper. Cook, stirring occasionally, until the Brussels sprouts are crisp and tender, about 5 minutes. Remove from the heat and stir in the lemon juice.

3 To serve, divide the rice among four bowls. Top with the Brussels sprouts, shredded carrot, radish, and Creamy Hummus, and sprinkle with the Hazelnut Dukkah.

Serves 4

1 cup (165 g) wild rice, rinsed
Kosher salt and freshly ground
   black pepper
1 tablespoon (15 ml) avocado
   or extra virgin olive oil
1 medium shallot, thinly sliced
1 pound (455 g) Brussels sprouts,
   trimmed and shredded
2 cloves garlic, minced
1½ teaspoons smoked paprika
Zest and juice of 1 lemon, divided
1 cup (110 g) shredded rainbow carrot
1 watermelon radish, thinly sliced
1 recipe Creamy Hummus (page 17)
¼ cup (35 g) Hazelnut Dukkah
   (page 24)

Get a head start! | The rice can be cooked a day in advance and reheated before serving.

BROTHY
BOWLS

Brothy Miso Mushroom Bowls

Calling all mushroom lovers! Enriched with a combination of dried and fresh mushrooms, plus a generous scoop of miso paste, these bowls start with a quick DIY mushroom broth that can be described as a umami bomb. It is sublimely savory, with a deep, balanced flavor. Then you have all of the goodies—toothsome brown rice, shredded cabbage, watercress, and tofu—that join forces to keep the bowls light, fresh, and filling.

Serves 4

½ ounce (14 g) dried porcini mushrooms

1 cup (240 ml) boiling water

2 tablespoons (30 ml) extra virgin olive oil

4 scallions, thinly sliced, whites and greens divided

1 pound (455 g) mixed mushrooms, such as cremini, shiitake, and oyster, sliced

¼ cup (60 g) white miso paste

3 cups (720 ml) low-sodium vegetable broth

2 cups (360 g) cooked brown rice

1 small bunch watercress, ends trimmed

1½ cups (105 g) finely shredded green cabbage

6 ounces (168 g) silken tofu, cut into ½-inch (1.3 cm) cubes

1 Place the dried mushrooms in a bowl, cover with the boiling water, and soak until just softened, about 20 minutes.

2 Meanwhile, heat the oil in a Dutch oven over medium heat until shimmering. Add the white part of the scallions and sauté until softened, about 2 minutes. Add the fresh mushrooms and cook, stirring occasionally, until softened, about 10 minutes. Add the miso paste and stir to coat the mushrooms until the miso is mostly dissolved. Pour in the broth, the reserved porcini mushrooms, and the mushroom liquid. Bring to a boil over medium-high heat, then reduce the heat and simmer for 15 minutes.

3 To serve, divide the rice, watercress, cabbage, and tofu among four bowls. Spoon the mushrooms over the top, followed by the broth. Garnish with the scallion greens.

Vegetable Ramen Bowls

If you ask me, really good ramen bowls start with really good broth. And that's where you'll put most of your efforts with this recipe. For maximum flavor, you'll start with a mix of vegetable broth and water, which gets enriched with browned onion and garlic, dried shiitakes, kombu, soy sauce, and mirin. The result is a rich and deeply nourishing base for your bowl, which is topped with a pile of noodles and a mess of fresh and cooked vegetables.

Serves 4

1 tablespoon (15 ml) avocado or extra virgin olive oil

1 medium onion, thinly sliced

2 cloves garlic, smashed

4 cups (960 ml) low-sodium vegetable broth

3 cups (720 ml) water

2 tablespoons (30 ml) soy sauce or tamari

2 tablespoons (30 ml) mirin

1 sheet dried kombu, rinsed

½ ounce (14 g) dried shiitake mushrooms

8 ounces (225 g) dry vegan ramen noodles

8 ounces (225 g) soft tofu, cubed

1 small bunch watercress, chopped

6 radishes, thinly sliced

1 cup (50 g) bean sprouts

1 Heat the oil in a Dutch oven or large, heavy-bottomed pot over medium heat until shimmering. Add the onion and garlic and sauté, stirring occasionally, until softened and lightly browned around the edges, 8 to 10 minutes. Pour in the vegetable broth and water, and scrape the browned bits from the bottom of the pot. Stir in the soy sauce, mirin, kombu, and dried shiitake mushrooms. Bring to a boil over medium-high heat, then reduce the heat to low and simmer for 30 minutes.

2 Strain the onions, mushrooms, garlic, and kombu from the broth. Remove and discard the garlic and kombu. Reserve the mushrooms and onions, then thinly slice the mushrooms.

3 Meanwhile, cook the ramen noodles in a separate pot according to the package instructions.

4 To serve, divide the noodles, reserved onions and mushrooms, tofu, watercress, radishes, and bean sprouts among four bowls. Pour the broth over the top.

Brothy Harissa-Spiced Butternut Squash and Chickpea Bowls

Loaded with seasoned melt-in-your-mouth cubes of butternut squash, hearty chickpeas, a mess of greens, and nutty millet, all just barely swimming in a spiced tomato and harissa-tinged broth, this bowl falls somewhere between a stew and a soup. It's deeply warming, totally nourishing, and a sprinkle of fresh cilantro on top keeps the whole thing feeling fresh.

1 Heat the oil in a Dutch oven or heavy-bottomed pot over medium heat until shimmering. Add the onion and sauté, stirring occasionally, until softened, about 5 minutes. Stir in the garlic, harissa and tomato pastes, coriander, cumin, cinnamon, a pinch of salt, and a few grinds of black pepper. Cook until fragrant, about 2 minutes. Stir in the butternut squash, chickpeas, broth, and tomatoes. Bring to a boil over medium-high heat, then reduce the heat to low and simmer until the squash is tender, about 30 minutes. Remove from the heat and stir in the spinach.

2 Meanwhile, combine the millet, water, and a pinch of salt in a medium saucepan. Bring to a boil over medium-high heat, then reduce the heat to low, cover, and simmer until the millet is tender and most of the water is absorbed, about 20 minutes. Remove from the heat and steam in the pot for 5 minutes.

3 To serve, divide the millet among four bowls. Top with the butternut squash and chickpea mixture and sprinkle with fresh cilantro leaves.

Serves 4

2 tablespoons (30 ml) avocado or extra virgin olive oil

1 small yellow onion, diced

2 cloves garlic, minced

1 teaspoon harissa paste

1 teaspoon tomato paste

2 teaspoons ground coriander

2 teaspoons ground cumin

½ teaspoon ground cinnamon

Kosher salt and freshly ground black pepper

1 pound (455 g) butternut squash, peeled, seeded, and cut into ½-inch (1.3 cm) cubes

1½ cups (360 g) or 1 (15-ounce [420 g]) can chickpeas, drained and rinsed

4 cups (960 ml) low-sodium vegetable broth

1 (28-ounce [784 g]) can fire-roasted crushed tomatoes

5 ounces (140 g) baby spinach

¾ cup (120 g) millet

2 cups (480 ml) water

¼ cup (4 g) fresh cilantro leaves

Green Curry Bowls

It's hard not to love the comforting combination of noodles swimming in a rich, fragrant curry broth. The steamy aroma alone is enough to entice you. Here, this brothy bowl starts with a big nest of zucchini noodles. The bite of the noodles is a welcome contrast to the tender eggplant and green beans simmered in the curry, and pick up hints of ginger and garlic. If you skip the precut zucchini noodles and spiralize them yourself, go ahead and chop up the vegetable's core, then toss it in the pot with the green beans and tofu. I prefer to use fresh green beans whenever possible, though frozen will also work—just hold off on adding them to the pot until the last 2 minutes of cooking.

1 Heat the oil in a Dutch oven over medium heat until shimmering. Add the garlic and ginger and cook until fragrant, about 30 seconds. Stir in the curry paste and cook for 2 minutes longer. Stir in the coconut milk, broth, and eggplant, and season with salt and a few grinds of black pepper. Bring to a boil over medium-high heat, then reduce the heat to low and simmer for 20 minutes. Stir in the tofu and green beans, and simmer for 10 minutes longer. Remove from the heat and stir in the lime juice.

2 To serve, divide the zucchini noodles among four bowls. Top with the eggplant, tofu, and green beans. Spoon the curry sauce over the top and garnish with the basil leaves and sliced chile (if using).

Serves 4

1 tablespoon (15 ml) coconut oil

3 cloves garlic, minced

1½ tablespoons (12 g) finely chopped fresh ginger

3 tablespoons (45 g) vegan Thai green curry paste

1 (14-ounce [392 g]) can unsweetened coconut milk

1 cup (240 ml) low-sodium vegetable broth

1 medium eggplant (about 1 pound [455 g]), cubed

Kosher salt and freshly ground black pepper

14 ounces (392 g) extra-firm tofu, drained and cubed

8 ounces (225 g) green beans, trimmed

Juice from ½ lime

1 pound (454 g) zucchini noodles

½ cup (30 g) fresh basil leaves

1 bird's eye chile, sliced (optional)

Kale and Tofu Curry Bowls

There's no shortage of ways to cook up a bunch of moody purple kale, but this bowl, inspired by Thai red curry, happens to be my favorite. It's packed with vitamins A and C, as well as potassium, calcium, and fiber, and a short simmer is just right to soften the otherwise tough leaves. If you can't find purple kale, a big bunch of curly green kale makes a fine substitute. Starting with a jar of curry paste is a smart shortcut that cuts down the ingredient list and simmer time, yet still leaves you with a flavor-packed bowl. Not all brands of curry paste are vegan, so be sure to check the label.

Serves 4

1½ tablespoons (23 ml) virgin coconut oil

2 shallots, thinly sliced

3 tablespoons (45 g) vegan Thai red curry paste

4 medium carrots, peeled and sliced

1½ cups (360 g) or 1 (15-ounce [420 g]) can chickpeas, drained and rinsed

1 (14-ounce [392 g]) can unsweetened coconut milk

1½ cups (360 ml) low-sodium vegetable broth

Kosher salt and freshly ground black pepper

14 ounces (392 g) extra-firm tofu, drained and cubed

1 large bunch purple kale, chopped

1 cup (175 g) tricolor quinoa, rinsed

1¾ cups (420 ml) water

⅓ cup (27 g) unsweetened toasted coconut flakes

¼ cup (4 g) fresh cilantro leaves

Lime wedges

1 Heat the oil in a Dutch oven over medium heat until shimmering. Add the shallot and cook until softened, about 2 minutes. Stir in the curry paste and cook until fragrant, about 2 minutes longer. Add the carrots, chickpeas, coconut milk, broth, a pinch of salt, and a few grinds of black pepper and stir to combine. Bring to a boil over medium-high heat, then reduce the heat to low and simmer for 20 minutes. Stir in the tofu and kale, and simmer for 10 minutes longer.

2 Meanwhile, place the quinoa, water, and a pinch of salt in a medium saucepan. Bring to a boil over medium-high heat, then reduce the heat to low, cover, and cook until tender, about 12 minutes. Remove from the heat and keep covered for 5 minutes. Fluff the quinoa with a fork.

3 To serve, divide the quinoa among four bowls. Top with the kale, tofu, and carrots. Spoon the curry sauce over the top and garnish with the coconut flakes, cilantro, and a lime wedge.

Get a head start! | The quinoa can be cooked a day in advance and reheated before serving.

Creamy Lemony White Bean Bowls with Greens

Comfort food can take on so many different forms, and these bowls are one of my favorites. Rich and hearty, they're as wholesome as they are comforting and warm you from the inside out. Pureeing a portion of the broth and beans leaves the mixture with an incredibly luxe, creamy texture without actually adding a drop of cream.

Serves 4

2 tablespoons (30 ml) avocado
    or extra virgin olive oil
1 medium yellow onion, diced
2 medium carrots, peeled and diced
2 ribs celery, diced
2 cloves garlic, minced
1 tablespoon (2 g) chopped fresh
    rosemary
Pinch of red pepper flakes, plus
    more for serving (optional)
Kosher salt and freshly ground
    black pepper
3 cups (720 ml) or 2 (15-ounce
    [420 g]) cans cannellini beans,
    drained and rinsed
3 cups (720 ml) low-sodium
    vegetable broth
1 bunch hearty greens, like kale,
    Swiss chard, or collard greens,
    leaves chopped
Finely grated zest and juice
    from 1 lemon
1 cup (175 g) tricolor quinoa
1¾ cups (420 ml) water
¼ cup (15 g) chopped fresh parsley
    leaves

1 Heat the oil in a Dutch oven or heavy-bottomed pot over medium heat until shimmering. Add the onion, carrots, and celery and sauté, stirring occasionally, until softened, 6 to 8 minutes. Add the garlic, rosemary, red pepper flakes, a pinch of salt, and a few grinds of black pepper and cook until fragrant, about 1 minute. Stir in the beans and broth. Bring to a boil over medium-high heat, then reduce the heat to low and simmer for 20 minutes.

2 Ladle 2 cups (480 ml), including vegetables, beans, and broth, into a blender and puree until smooth. Return to the pot, along with the greens, lemon zest, and juice. Cover and steam for 5 minutes.

3 Meanwhile, place the quinoa, water, and a pinch of salt in a medium saucepan. Bring to a boil over medium-high heat, reduce the heat to low, cover, and cook until tender, about 12 minutes. Remove from the heat and keep covered for 5 minutes. Fluff the quinoa with a fork.

4 To serve, divide the quinoa among four bowls. Ladle the white bean mixture over the top and sprinkle with the fresh parsley and extra red pepper flakes, if desired.

Soothing Ginger Turmeric Broth Bowls

Anytime I feel like I might be coming down with something or I just want a meal that feels healing and completely nourishing, these ginger- and turmeric-infused broth bowls are the first place I turn. Packed with vegetables, rice, and chickpeas, they have a warm, gentle taste that puts my body at ease. The recipe calls for fresh turmeric, which you'll peel and mince as you would fresh ginger; it acts as an anti-inflammatory and has a bright orange color beneath its skin, with an earthy, peppery taste.

1 Heat the oil in a Dutch oven or large pot over medium heat until shimmering. Add the shallot, garlic, ginger, turmeric, a pinch of salt, and a few grinds of black pepper and sauté until softened, about 5 minutes. Stir in the broth, scraping the bottom of the pot. Add the chickpeas, carrots, cauliflower, and rice. Bring to a boil over medium-high heat, then reduce the heat and simmer until the rice and vegetables are tender, 12 to 15 minutes. Remove from the heat and stir in the lime juice.

2 To serve, divide the baby spinach among four bowls. Ladle the rice, vegetables, and broth into the bowls and top with the fresh cilantro. Let it sit for a minute or two before serving, so the broth can soften the spinach.

Serves 4

2 tablespoons (30 ml) avocado
   or extra virgin olive oil
2 medium shallots, thinly sliced
3 cloves garlic, minced
1 tablespoon (8 g) finely minced
   fresh ginger
1 tablespoon (8 g) peeled and finely
   minced fresh turmeric root
Kosher salt and freshly ground
   black pepper
4 cups (960 ml) low-sodium
   vegetable broth
3 cups (720 ml) or 2 (15-ounce [420 g])
   chickpeas, drained and rinsed
3 medium carrots, peeled and cut
   into ½-inch (1.3 cm) pieces
½ head cauliflower, cut into bite-size
   florets
¾ cup (120 g) jasmine rice
Juice from 2 limes
5 ounces (140 g) baby spinach
¼ cup (4 g) chopped fresh cilantro
   leaves and tender stems

SWEET
BOWLS

Vanilla Chia Bowls

If you have a thing for vanilla bean ice cream, like I have a thing for vanilla bean ice cream, these chia pudding bowls will be right up your alley. Made with homemade cashew milk and vanilla bean paste, sweetened with dates, and kissed with a hint of sweet cinnamon, these bowls have a warm, sweet aroma and come speckled with hints of vanilla bean seed. I recommend using vanilla bean paste, which is easier (and less expensive) than scraping seeds from a pod and adds a more intense flavor than extract.

Serves 4

1 cup (145 g) raw cashews
1 tablespoon (15 g) vanilla bean paste
3 cups (720 ml) filtered water, plus
   more for soaking
6 pitted Medjool dates
½ teaspoon ground cinnamon
¼ teaspoon kosher salt
½ cup (70 g) chia seeds
8 fresh figs, halved
¼ cup (35 g) toasted hazelnuts,
   chopped
2 tablespoons (10 g) unsweetened
   toasted shredded coconut

1 Place the cashews in a jar or bowl, cover with water, and soak for at least 3 hours and up to overnight. Drain.

2 Place the cashews, vanilla bean paste, filtered water, dates, cinnamon, and salt in a blender and process on high speed until creamy and smooth, 3 to 5 minutes. Pour the liquid into a large bowl, then slowly whisk in the chia seeds and continue mixing until well distributed. Cover and refrigerate overnight.

3 To serve, stir together once more, then divide among four bowls. Top with the fresh figs, toasted hazelnuts, and toasted shredded coconut.

Whipped Pineapple-Coconut Bowls

You're not wrong if you think this ingredient list looks pretty similar to a smoothie. That's where the inspiration for this frozen tropical fruit bowl came from. What sets it apart, though, is that this sweet treat has a thickness that is closer to soft serve, with a little extra richness thanks to canned coconut milk.

1 Add the pineapple, banana, and agave to a food processor fitted with the blade attachment. Process just until the fruit is crumbly. Stop to scrape down the sides of the bowl. With the motor running, slowly pour in the coconut milk and process until smooth and creamy.

2 To serve immediately, divide the nice cream among four bowls. Top with chopped kiwi, fresh raspberries, and toasted coconut flakes. If not serving immediately, transfer to a lidded airtight container and freeze.

Serves 4

10 ounces (280 g) frozen pineapple chunks

1 banana, peeled, cut into chunks, and frozen

1 tablespoon (15 ml) agave nectar or pure maple syrup

1 cup (240 ml) unsweetened full-fat coconut milk

To serve
Chopped kiwi
Raspberries
Unsweetened toasted coconut flakes

Wintery Coconut Yogurt Bowls

These bowls are a celebration of the best part of winter—all the sweet (and bitter) citrus fruits, which are piled atop an airy pillow of whipped coconut yogurt. This recipe requires a little planning, as you'll want to chill the coconut milk in the fridge overnight. A quick blast in the freezer doesn't work quite as well—I've tried. You'll also want to chill the whipped yogurt before spooning everything into bowls.

Serves 4

1 (14-ounce [392 g]) can unsweetened full-fat coconut milk

1 cup (240 g) unsweetened coconut yogurt

2 teaspoons pure maple syrup

¼ cup (40 g) buckwheat

1 Cara Cara or navel orange, peeled

1 blood orange, peeled

1 medium grapefruit, peeled

¼ cup (35 g) pomegranate arils

¼ cup (20 g) unsweetened toasted coconut flakes

Fresh mint leaves, for garnish (optional)

1 Chill the can of coconut milk in the refrigerator overnight. Scoop ½ cup (120 g) of hardened coconut cream from the top of the can. Reserve the remaining cream and liquid for smoothies or cooking rice or grains (remember this last part, you can thank me later!).

2 Add the coconut cream, yogurt, and maple syrup to a large bowl and beat with an electric mixer on high speed (or in a stand mixer with the whisk attachment) until airy and increased in volume, about 2 minutes. Chill for at least 1 hour and up to overnight to firm up.

3 Meanwhile, toast the buckwheat in a dry skillet over medium-low heat, stirring occasionally, until fragrant and lightly browned all over, 5 to 8 minutes. Set aside to cool completely.

4 Slice the citrus fruits crosswise into rounds, then pull apart into smaller segments.

5 To serve, divide the citrus segments among four bowls. Top with spoonfuls of the whipped yogurt, followed by the pomegranate arils, toasted buckwheat, coconut flakes, and mint leaves (if using).

Get a head start! | The coconut yogurt mixture can be prepared up to a day in advance and stored in the refrigerator. The buckwheat can be toasted in advance, and once cool, stored in an airtight container for several weeks.

PB&J Nice Cream Bowls

This cool and refreshing dessert bowl brings together the best of two worlds: a classic PB&J sandwich and banana "ice cream." You'll serve the peanut butter–banana nice cream straight from the food processor when it has a lush consistency similar to soft serve, then you'll top off your bowl with glossy stewed berries, crushed peanuts, and a nutty seed sprinkle. When freezing the bananas, I recommend cutting them into slices no larger than 1 inch (2.5 cm) thick. Not only is it easier on your food processor, but the bananas also break down faster and more evenly.

1 Place the berries and maple syrup in a small saucepan over medium heat and cook, stirring regularly and breaking up the berries with the back of a spoon, until the berries have burst and the mixture is slightly thickened, about 5 minutes. Set aside to cool completely.

2 Add the frozen bananas to a food processor fitted with the blade attachment. Process just until the bananas are crumbly. Stop to scrape down the sides of the bowl and add the peanut butter. With the motor running, slowly pour in the nut milk and process until smooth and creamy.

3 To serve immediately, divide the nice cream among four bowls. Top with the berry compote, peanuts, and Sweet Seed Sprinkle. If not serving immediately, transfer to a lidded airtight container and freeze.

Serves 4

1½ cups (225 g) blueberries, fresh or frozen

2 tablespoons (30 ml) pure maple syrup

4 medium bananas, peeled, sliced, and frozen

¾ cup (180 g) smooth natural peanut butter

¾ cup (180 ml) unsweetened cashew or almond milk

¼ cup (35 g) chopped unsalted roasted peanuts

¼ cup (35 g) Sweet Seed Sprinkle (page 16)

Get a head start! | The stewed berries can be cooked in advance and stored in an airtight container in the refrigerator until serving.

Chocolate Avocado Pudding

Judging by the rich creaminess and deep chocolaty flavor of this pudding, it's more than likely you'll forget that it's a totally wholesome dessert. Want to amp up the chocolate flavor even more? Start with a container of chocolate milk rather than the regular stuff. Make a mental note to plan ahead for this one because the can of coconut milk, which you'll use for a pillowy topping, needs to chill in the fridge overnight so the cream can firm up. Since you'll only use a ½ cup (120 g) of the coconut cream, I recommend reserving the remaining cream and liquid for smoothies or cooking rice or grains.

Serves 4

2 ripe avocados
¼ cup (30 g) unsweetened cocoa
   powder
¼ cup (60 ml) agave nectar or pure
   maple syrup
¼ cup (60 ml) unsweetened nondairy
   milk, regular or chocolate
1 teaspoon pure vanilla extract
Pinch of kosher salt
1 (14-ounce [392 g]) can unsweetened
   full-fat coconut milk, refrigerated
   overnight
1 tablespoon (8 g) powdered sugar
   (optional)
Fresh raspberries, for serving

1 Scoop out the avocado flesh and add to the bowl of a food processor fitted with the blade attachment, along with the cocoa powder, agave, milk, vanilla, and salt. Blend until smooth, scraping down the sides of the bowl as necessary.

2 Divide among four bowls, cover, and refrigerate for at least 30 minutes before serving.

3 Scoop ½ cup (120 g) of hardened coconut cream from the top of the can. Add to a large bowl and beat with an electric mixer on high speed (or in a stand mixer fitted with the whisk attachment) until airy and small peaks have formed, about 2 minutes. If using, add the powdered sugar and beat until incorporated.

4 To serve, top each bowl with a dollop of coconut whipped cream and fresh raspberries.

Caramelized Banana Bowls

Ready to take bananas from work-a-day snack to impossibly mouthwatering and wholesome dessert? All it takes is giving a quick sear in a coconut oil–slicked skillet plus a drizzle of agave and a pinch of sweet cinnamon. Serve the bananas over a bed of your favorite nondairy yogurt, and be sure not to forget the seedy topping. Stick with firm bananas, even ones that aren't fully ripe yet—the heat softens them and draws out the fruit's natural sweetness.

1 Heat the coconut oil in a large nonstick skillet over medium-high heat until shimmering. Add the bananas and cook for 2 minutes. Flip the bananas, drizzle with the agave, sprinkle with the cinnamon, and cook for 2 to 3 minutes longer.

2 To serve, divide the bananas among four bowls, top with a scoop of yogurt, and garnish with the Sweet Seed Sprinkle.

Serves 4

2 tablespoons (30 ml) virgin coconut oil

3 medium-large firm, ripe bananas, halved lengthwise and cut into 2-inch (5 cm) pieces

2 tablespoons (30 ml) agave nectar or pure maple syrup

½ teaspoon ground cinnamon

1 cup (240 g) unsweetened nondairy yogurt

¼ cup (35 g) Sweet Seed Sprinkle (page 16)

Chai-Poached Pears with Cashew Crumble

Be prepared to fall in love with this sweet dessert long before you even take a bite. As the pears simmer, and again as you reduce the tea-spiked cooking liquid into a drizzly syrup, your kitchen will be perfumed with the scent of warm spices, like cinnamon, ginger, and cardamom. You might even catch a hint of maple. If the idea of doubling the cashew crumble crossed your mind, so you have something fun to spoon over your yogurt in the morning, go with it.

Serves 4

½ cup (50 g) old-fashioned
   rolled oats
¼ cup (30 g) almond flour
2 tablespoons (16 g) chopped raw
   cashews
⅛ teaspoon ground cinnamon
⅛ teaspoon ground ginger
Pinch of kosher salt
2 tablespoons (30 ml) virgin
   coconut oil
4 tablespoons (60 ml) pure maple
   syrup, divided
4 cups (960 ml) water
4 chai tea bags
4 firm pears (preferably Bosc),
   peeled, halved lengthwise,
   and cored

Get a head start! | The cashew crumble can be made in advance and stored in an airtight container until you're ready to serve.

1 Preheat the oven to 350°F (180°C or gas mark 4). Line a baking sheet with parchment paper.

2 In a large bowl, mix together the oats, almond flour, cashews, cinnamon, ginger, and salt. Pour in the coconut oil and 2 tablespoons (30 ml) of the maple syrup, then stir to coat the dry ingredients. Spread in an even layer on the prepared baking sheet. Bake until golden brown and crisp, 15 to 20 minutes. Let cool completely.

3 Bring the water to a boil in a large saucepan. Remove from the heat, add the tea bags, and steep for 5 minutes. Squeeze the remaining liquid from the tea bags and remove from the pan. Return the pan to the heat, stir in the remaining 2 tablespoons (30 ml) maple syrup, and bring the liquid to a simmer. Reduce the heat to low, add the pears, cover, and cook until the pears are tender, 15 to 20 minutes. Remove the pears with a slotted spoon and set aside.

4 Bring the poaching liquid to a boil and cook until slightly thickened and syrupy, 5 to 7 minutes.

5 To serve, divide the poached pears among four bowls. Spoon the chai syrup over the top and sprinkle with the crumble.

Coconut Chia Bowls

Chia pudding is usually an all-day treat in my book, but the rich and creamy canned coconut milk that gets stirred into this version leaves it squarely in dessert territory. It's flavored with warm vanilla extract and nutmeg, which just might remind you of the tropics, and topped with sliced banana, toasty cacao nibs, and walnuts.

1 Add the milks, yogurt, agave, vanilla, nutmeg, and salt to a large bowl. Stir well until smooth. Slowly whisk in the chia seeds and continue mixing until well distributed. Cover and refrigerate overnight.

2 To serve, stir together once more, then divide among four bowls. Top with the sliced banana, toasted walnuts, and cacao nibs.

Serves 4

1 cup (240 ml) light unsweetened canned coconut milk

1 cup (240 ml) unsweetened nondairy milk

½ cup (120 g) unsweetened coconut yogurt

2 tablespoons (30 ml) agave nectar or pure maple syrup

2 teaspoons pure vanilla extract

¼ teaspoon ground nutmeg

¼ teaspoon kosher salt

½ cup (70 g) chia seeds

1 banana, sliced

⅓ cup (35 g) chopped toasted walnuts

2 tablespoons (16 g) cacao nibs

Tropical Fruit Bowls

To anyone who argues that fruit isn't dessert, tropical fruit bowls will make you a believer. My secret to making fruit feel like a special, if not indulgent, dessert is using fruits I don't typically eat on a regular basis. Drizzled with a lime-agave dressing and topped with toasted coconut flakes, these bowls will be quick to remind you of the tropics, which feels like an especially wonderful treat in the middle of winter.

Serves 4

¼ cup (60 ml) freshly squeezed lime
    juice (about 2 limes)
Zest of 2 limes
1 tablespoon (15 ml) agave nectar
½ small papaya, trimmed, seeded,
    and cubed
½ small pineapple, trimmed, cored,
    and cubed
1 mango, peeled, pitted, and chopped
1 dragon fruit (pitaya), trimmed
    and cubed
¼ cup (20 g) unsweetened toasted
    coconut flakes

1 Place the lime juice, zest, and agave in a small jar with a tight-fitting lid. Close and shake until the agave is dissolved. If not using immediately, store in the refrigerator until ready to use.

2 Divide the fruit among four bowls. Drizzle with the lime dressing and top with the toasted coconut flakes.

ACKNOWLEDGMENTS

To my editor Dan Rosenberg, as well as the entire team at Harvard Common Press and Quarto: Thank you for coaching me along and, most of all, for bringing this project to life.

To Maria Siriano: Many, many thanks once again for capturing my vision so beautifully.

To the Kitchn team: You all constantly inspire me and make me a better writer and person. I'm truly lucky to work with such a smart and talented group.

To my family and friends: Your endless support, love, encouragement, and willingness to taste and test my recipes mean the world to me. I could not have done this without you.

And, finally, to Lucien: I couldn't have done this without you. You have been my dishwasher, taste tester, and number one supporter every step of the way. Thank you for always believing in me and pushing me to follow my dreams.

ABOUT THE AUTHOR

Kelli Foster is a food writer, recipe developer, and author of the cookbooks *Buddha Bowls* and *The Probiotic Kitchen*. She is a longtime editor at the popular cooking site Kitchn. Her writing and recipes can be found in numerous online and print publications, including Greatist, Clean Plates, and *Triathlete Magazine*.

INDEX

PLANT-BASED BUDDHA BOWLS